MY WONDERFUL WORLD OF GOLF

Toney Penna (H. L. Hoss)

MY WONDERFUL WORLD OF

Toney Penna

with Oscar Fraley

centaur house/inc.
New York City

Distributed by Hawthorn Books, Inc.

Copyright © 1965 by Centaur House, Inc. All rights reserved, including the right to reproduce this book or portions thereof in any form. All inquiries should be addressed to Hawthorn Books, Inc., 70 Fifth Avenue, New York City 10011. This book was manufactured in the United States of America and published simultaneously in Canada by Prentice-Hall of Canada, Ltd., 520 Ellesmere Road, Scarborough, Ontario. Library of Congress Catalog Card Number: 65-22905.

First Edition, November, 1965

To "Imp"

The lovely lady I met in Pensacola and who, through the intervening years, as my wife has put up with so much to help me carve my niche in the game of golf.

FOREWORD

If there is any one man to whom golf owes a tremendous debt it would have to be my long-time friend, Toney Penna.

In the modern era of production-line golf, with week after week of tournaments whose purses make King Midas look like a penny pincher, everybody knows such players as Arnold Palmer, Jack Nicklaus, Tony Lima, Billy Casper, *et al.* They are household words.

And yet I have to feel that thirty years ago the missionary work which was done produced the golden product of today.

Toney Penna was in the forefront of these pioneers.

He was, and still is, a fiery and intense little man whose whole being was concentrated on selling the game of golf. I was fortunate enough to travel with him in those earlier times but most of us concentrated on the fun side of the fairway.

Toney was always selling: pride in the profession, the MacGregor clubs, which he completely redesigned, current and future tournament sponsors, headline names whose glamour would attract others to golf and, above everything else, the game of golf, which he loves with such tremendous devotion.

As a player, he was the toughest type of competitor. Penna was gifted with one of the soundest, most beautifully uncomplicated swings I have ever seen. If there was a flaw in his game it was on the putting greens.

Back then when we traveled together the tour was a sometime thing. Tournaments were widely scattered across the calendar and we did not compete with enough regularity to match the human scoring machines of today. He did, however, win a number of championships, while I was fortunate enough to take the Masters three times.

I mention this merely to put across the point that we had our fair share of players and that Toney stood high in our ranks.

I cannot overemphasize his thorough understanding of the game of golf during an era in which theories and techniques were not always eye to eye.

Together we had many humorous experiences and yet when I think of Penna I remember him as a man with great pride in himself, in the game and in the people who enjoyed "his" sport. The word for him is "dedication."

Always he had an eye for the superfine, whether it was clothing, talent in others or the type of convert who could help the game of golf another step forward.

The players of today are rarely on close and intimate terms with their following, club members or tournament sponsors. It is not their fault. They are too busy jumping from tournament to tournament and capitalizing on vast outside interests.

This job, however, has long since been taken care of

for them by men such as Penna, who fraternized and socialized the game into a major industry. Thus was the tour set into the laps of the current crop of tournament stars on a silver platter.

Much of the thanks should go to Toney Penna: super player, salesman, club designer, missionary and friend to golfers everywhere. The game of golf owes him a debt it can never repay.

JIMMY DEMARET
Houston, Texas
May 23, 1965

CONTENTS

Foreword by Jimmy Demaret	7
Tailoring Your Clubs	13
I Learn the Game	41
Gusty Memories	79
Of Men, No Mice	97
The Celebri-tees	111
"Doctoring" the Pros	129
Pro-Type Tips	143
For the Beginner	173
My All-Time Top Ten	201
Mind Your Manners	223
The Authors and Their Book	240

ILLUSTRATIONS

Toney Penna	*Frontispiece*
Jack Burke, Toney Penna, Jimmy Demaret	21
Toney Penna, Clarence Custonborder, Bob Lysaugh	27
Tommy Armour	49
Clarence Rickey	61
Toney Penna, Bob Lysaugh, Clarence Custonborder	71
Toney Penna, Mickey Rooney, Fred Astaire	87
Ben Hogan	105
Phil Harris, Bing Crosby	115
Perry Como, Toney Penna	119
Bo Wininger, Frank Sinatra, Toney Penna	125
Sam Snead	135
Arnold Palmer	163
Bobby Jones	183
Gene Sarazen	189
Jack Nicklaus	205
Toney Penna, Bing Crosby, Frank Sinatra	215
Gary Player	219
Toney Penna	235

TAILORING YOUR CLUBS

The odds are probably as high as ten to one that you are using a set of golf clubs which aren't suited to you.

Just to get my point across, you wouldn't use a tack hammer to drive a railroad spike nor would you use a twenty-pound sledge hammer to set a thumb tack.

To get the absolute in efficiency out of your set it must have "feel" and playability.

In obtaining these two vitally essential factors you must have clubs which fit your own particular size and strength.

The ingredients are the correct type of shaft which will react perfectly to the power of your swing; a grip which feels comfortable to you; the proper lie of the clubhead for your height, and a selected swing weight which will get the clubhead into the ball perfectly for the speed of your swing.

I do not say this because I am a club designer for MacGregor, whose business is selling golf clubs. The fact is, quite simply, that I love this game and thoroughly enjoy seeing people play it well. It frustrates me when I observe players failing to make progress because they are using the wrong tools.

If you are one of those sufferers who are shy of control, who have an erratic touch or who feel that they are not getting the distance they deserve or should generate, then I would have to guess that it probably is due to the fact that you and your clubs are mismated.

In this chapter I am going to attempt to explain the many and varied facets of a golf club to you. My reasoning is that if you have a general knowledge of what makes a club feel perfect to one person and not to another then you will have at least a working idea of how to assay your own difficulties.

Along these lines, there is an accompanying chart which, generally speaking, outlines the manner in which clubs should be tailored to various individuals.

There are, of course, exceptions to every rule and your smartest move would be to put yourself into the hands of an able golf professional who has the experience and the ability necessary to fit you perfectly. Bear in mind, too, that he will be laboring under somewhat of a handicap unless he knows your game or the speed of your swing.

However, just to provide you with a general understanding of what you should be seeking, let's start first with the shaft, which actually is the heart of the golf club.

You must face the fact right at the beginning that if

you don't have a shaft which suits your swing speed you do not have a playable golf club no matter how handsome it may look on the rack.

Starting out basically, the larger the diameter of the shaft, the stiffer it will be. The smaller the diameter of the shaft, the more supple it becomes. This bending or whipping action of the shaft during the swing is known as flex and there are many different degrees of flex.

Some clubs are built with the flex near the head area of the club, giving you a bit more flip of the head at the bottom of the swing providing you have the power to make it work. The most popular shaft is where the flex is focalized in the center.

How does this affect you?

Well, if you are a very strong and able player such as Arnold Palmer or Jack Nicklaus, you require a stiff shaft to handle your power. On the other hand, if you are an average player of average strength, you cannot physically generate the power necessary to make the club they use release its whipping power for you. Thus you would need the number two shaft.

But let's say that the years are creeping up on you as you enter your fifties or sixties. Your ability may be lessening, your foot action may be slowing down, and possibly you no longer can turn at the ball as you did in your younger years. This means that the regular shaft will not whip for you as it did formerly.

All is not lost. For the number three shaft, with its greater whip, will make compensation for these deficits.

One point which must be taken into consideration along these lines is that if you wind up with too much flex, then control of the ball becomes much more difficult. However, by changing the strength of your shaft with proper experimentation you can attain the perfect flex for your swing through the hitting area, which in the end is the most important area of the golf swing.

Take into account that when your hands enter the hitting area the shaft is bent almost like a buggy whip. Should a powerful player use a soft shaft, the clubhead would never catch up to the hands or it might fly on through the hitting area too rapidly. If an elderly person uses too stiff a shaft he simply is not able to get any whip action from the shaft. A good indication of whether you are in this category is that if the shaft you are playing is too stiff, your ball in flight will have too low a trajectory.

Moving along to another facet, you probably have heard a great deal of talk concerning swing weight.

Its purpose is merely to focalize the flex area of the shaft.

The heavier the swing weight, the lower the flex area is located on the shaft. The lighter the swing weight, the higher the flex area is on the shaft.

So we return to the principle that a weak person cannot make a club with a too heavy swing weight flex at the bottom of the shaft. As the swing weight is decreased, therefore, and the flex area moves up the shaft, it requires less power on the part of the player to make the club whip.

Normal swing weights range from the least flex resistance of C4, which is seldom used, to a strong flex resistance of D5, although in abnormal cases the swing weight goes as high as E4.

Running up from C4, swing weight is determined through measurement on a calibration machine which merely shows how the flex area is being moved down the shaft toward the clubhead, thereby designating the balance point of any particular club.

SWING WEIGHT CHART

FOR MEN

Shaft	Player	Swing Weight Range	Average
Extra stiff	Exceptionally tall or strong	D5 to E4	D5
#1 stiff	Strong, normal height	D2 to D5	D4
#2 regular	Average	D1 to D4	D2-D3
#3 soft	Elderly or less strong	D0 to D2	D1

FOR WOMEN

#3 regular	Strong	C7 to D1	C9
#4 soft	Less strong	C5 to C8	C5-C6

(*Swing weights range as high as E4 but their use is suggested only in extreme cases. A minimum of overall weight, referred to in the trade as "static weight," is very important in attaining these swing weights.*)

Speaking in generalities, you can see by observing and analyzing our accompanying chart how the type of shaft and the swing weight change as you move up the scale.

Thus a woman who is not exceptionally strong needs

all the whip in the shaft that she can obtain. This is because she does not have the power in her hands to make the shaft buggywhip and drive the released flexing power into the ball. It is obvious, therefore, that she would be better fitted with a number four soft shaft with anywhere from a C5 to a C6 swing weight which would give her maximum flex and proper balance to obtain the utmost efficiency from her clubs.

Your clubs, it follows, all should be swing-weighted similarly so that each one has the same feel when you are swinging.

Naturally the length of your clubs enters into this.

The standard driver is 43 inches long. The two wood is the same length. The three wood is 42½ inches and the four wood is 42 inches in length. The average irons range from 38½ inches for the two iron, graduating downward one-half inch in the length of each club all the way to the nine iron and wedge.

Ladies' clubs are one-half inch shorter all the way through the set.

Indicative again of how necessary it is to tailor your clubs to your own particular size and strength, George Bayer, one of MacGregor's touring stars, stands six feet, five inches tall and weighs 240 pounds. He uses a 44-inch driver, which is only one inch longer than the normal driver. Yet a man of his size who had shorter arms might require a driver 45 inches in length.

However, a short man with long arms may need to be tailored for clubs which are of ladies' length. In this case, providing he is of average strength, he should not

Jack Burke, Toney Penna, Jimmy Demaret, 1965 Buick Open
(Russ Scott)

settle for a swing weight of less than D1.

In this era of power hitting those who play golf have become more and more distance conscious. Naturally clubhead speed has a great deal to do with how far the ball can be struck. Yet this is not the true answer to being able to hit the ball farther.

The heavier the swing weight you can handle, the more distance you will be able to attain.

Yet you must be careful not to attempt to use a swing weight which is too heavy for you or you will not be able to get the ball up properly. The flex of the shaft as you whip in the clubhead causes the ball to get up into the air. A woman who is not extremely strong couldn't hope to play with a powerful shaft simply because she cannot get it to flex for her. As a man gets older, he naturally needs a more supple shaft to help him get the ball airborne.

But, as I said, weight is the answer to distance. Consider it this way. If you swing a club 90 miles per hour with a D2 swing weight it stands to reason that if you can swing a D8 at the same speed the increased weight is going to knock the ball farther. However, you always must be careful that you are not attempting to use too heavy a swing weight because you may be cutting down on the speed of your swing or failing to make the club flex and, in the process, you will be losing distance.

Therefore, getting your maximum distance results from a combination of the greatest speed which you can generate with your swing added to the maximum swing weight which you can handle.

The grip of the club naturally has a great deal to do with its swing weight. A heavier grip will produce a lighter swing weight. A lighter or smaller grip will produce a heavier swing weight.

Yet bear in mind that the size of the grip should be determined solely by your own individual feel.

In explanation, I've seen a large man such as Tommy Armour use what appears to be a ladies' grip even though he has a large, powerful pair of hands. Yet, in my own case, even though my hands are strong they are very small and still I use an extra large grip.

So it is the grip that feels best to you which you should use. The size of your hands has absolutely nothing to do with which type of club grip you select. Bear in mind that you want the one which feels best.

Another good example is Jack Nicklaus. For a large man he has an extremely small, though powerful, pair of hands. Yet he uses a larger than standard size grip. This also is one of the reasons why in taking his grip on the club he uses the interlocking grip, but we will go into various methods of gripping the club later.

Still another vitally important factor in selecting your clubs is to be certain that they have the proper lie for your size. By "lie" I mean that when you comfortably address the ball the sole of the clubhead should be flat or level with the ground.

The lie of the club for the tall person must be on the upright side because, being taller, he stands closer to the ball and the club must be more upright to him to sole the club on the ground properly. There is, of course, a valid reason for making certain that the lie is proper.

If a golf club is too upright for you, meaning that the heel touches the ground while the outside toe comes up off the ground at address, you will have a tendency to create a hook. On the opposite extreme, if the club is not upright enough, the heel will be up off the ground and the toe will be down, setting up a tendency to slice the ball.

When selecting your woods, one of the most essential considerations is the degree to which they have been bored. Most standard woods are bored with two degrees of hook which permits you to address the ball perfectly straight. The reason is that if it was bored absolutely straight the club would appear toed off and have a tendency to throw your hands behind the clubhead. You can get a wood bored with as much as four degrees of hook, meaning that the toe of the club will be toed in toward the ball. Thus if you have a tendency to slice then it behooves you to get clubs bored with more degrees of hook. On the other aspect, if you are a hooker, you want a club bored to a smaller degree.

The standard set of irons is bored perfectly straight. The reason here is that the hosel, the necklike projection from the clubhead, has been set up in front of the sole line of the club.

At MacGregor we proudly claim that we produce the Cadillac of golf clubs in our three top lines. These are the Tommy Armour line, the MacGregor Tourney or

MT line and the DX line, the latter being engineering abbreviation for distance.

Why three top lines?

We have these three lines because they have individual differences and thereby satisfy all types of personal preferences.

Talk to any group of players and you will hear some of them say they prefer a thin top line. Others want a thick top line which gives them a feeling of playing a more powerful club while still others demand something in between.

Our Tommy Armour line has a slightly deeper blade, about one-sixteenth of an inch more than most clubs on the market, and a medium thick top line. Playability still remains ideal because the playability of a golf club originates on the sole line. This sole line strength is concentrated about six-eighths to seven-eighths of an inch up in the middle of the face of the club.

The MT line has a plain and yet very functional type of back. The beauty of the MT is that the whole face is solid hitting area, meaning that there is no focal area or "sweet spot" where the ball must be hit to utilize the strength of the club. Anytime you hit the ball on the face of the club you have power behind it. This one factor alone, to my mind, makes it the most functional club on the market for the average player.

Our DX line is, to my way of thinking, one of the most beautiful on the market. This DX line focalizes the hitting area with the weight distribution well located for added distance. Visually, the back is one of the most attractive you can find while remaining extremely functional.

However, in all three lines, as far as playability is concerned they all have the same type of "engine" and capabilities, because playability is the primary thought to all of us at MacGregor when we think of constructing or creating a golf club. We hold that the customer must obtain the ultimate result possible or he isn't going to stick with our clubs. Eye appeal, what I refer to as visuality, is highly important, of course. Yet beyond this built-in beauty the club must function to perfection.

I have been asked many times how we go about designing new clubs. I can sum it up in three letters: O-R-C.

O-R-C for more than thirty years with MacGregor has been my business Bible. It stands for observing, remembering and comparing.

You would be surprised how many tips of extreme value can be picked up just listening to professionals when they are chatting about golf clubs. For example, a good many years back we had but one flex of golf shaft. It was through the suggestion of pros I called on throughout the country that we finally introduced all types of flexes in golf shafts. It provided us, also, with a slogan:

"Play the clubs the pros built."

Whenever I get an idea, whether it happens to be my own or one suggested to me in a conversation, I

Toney Penna, Clarence Custonborder, Bob Lysaugh at the
MacGregor broach machine (MacGregor)

head back to the plant or to my shop at home to work on it privately and determine whether it may be an improvement over what we already have.

In the early days I experimented by using a file and a sanding wheel. Later we worked in plastics and now we are using a plastic steel which is malleable and easy to work with.

Once the idea has been transposed into steel, we make up an actual polished working model at the factory.

Through every step of this experimentation the man I'm thinking of is the duffer, the 95-and-up shooter. Thus our paramount idea has to commence with playability, which is obtained in an iron club by weight distribution.

For example, weight distribution on a long iron must be at the lowest possible point. The strongest part of the club must be from within six-eighths to seven-eighths of an inch from the sole line, that part of the club which is in contact with the turf. If it isn't, no matter what type of head you may like, you do not have a good, strong, playable golf club. Thus your weight distribution must be strong from that six- to seven-eighths of an inch up from the sole line and must move fractionally up the face as the loft of the iron increases.

Another factor which is involved is that we must be extremely careful with the scoring of our clubs, meaning the lines which run horizontally across the face of the blade. If these lines were made extremely deep, anyone could stop the ball on a dime because the backspin created would be so severe. Therefore the United States Golf Association has put a limit on the depth of this scoring.

Their ruling came after Jock Hutchison won the British Open with a very severely ribbed club called a spade mashie, a club with which he was able to make the ball do circus tricks.

The hosel, the neck which protrudes from the head and by which it is joined to the shaft, also must meet rigid specifications established by the U.S.G.A. The juncture of shaft and hosel is finished over with what is called an adaptor but this is done simply in the interest of eye appeal.

As I have pointed out previously, our first concern in making a golf club is playability. Ordinarily this is of little interest to the customer. He takes it for granted that if MacGregor or any other major company puts a club on the market it of necessity will be playable.

Thus it is that visuality, eye appeal, plays a major role in creating new merchandise. In this connection, we at MacGregor pioneered the use of color in golf clubs.

As an example, when I went to work for MacGregor the company had a line called the Black Scot, which was Tommy Armour's personal origination. But when Tommy's hair turned silver, seemingly overnight, we changed the name to "Silver Scot" and introduced a new line with a chrome-plated shaft and even a silver-beaded grip. This sold me utterly and irrevocably on the necessity of built-in eye appeal.

Searching always for perfection, we at MacGregor were the first to introduce the broaching machine into the industry. Prior to this we used various methods but we would not be satisfied with anything less than microscopic uniformity. The broaching machine, a hydraulic machine with cutters, enabled us actually to shave steel in a flawlessly straight manner.

Immediately after World War II we introduced our MT line and it was a brand-new concept in golf clubs. The MT had the most compact and smallest blade ever put on the market, and most clubs today still are made in this same compact fashion. Making the MT iron provided us at MacGregor with another "first," introduction of the milling machine into the industry. It is similar to the broaching machine but, where the latter shaves in a straight line, the milling machine follows contours with that same microscopic precision we had been seeking.

When we introduced the MT line, we decided to give it eye appeal by placing an MT insignia on the back of the club.

"What's this?" one pro asked me. "It looks like something out of a Chinese laundry."

I explained, with maybe just a trace of irritation, that it was an M with a T over the top of it, standing for MacGregor Tourney.

"Well," he conceded, "it does make it look slick."

Our next step, and one which was to have a far-reaching effect on the industry, was to start the coloring of golf clubs.

My idea was to set up the hitting area of the club face with color, a touchy project because of the United States Golf Association's rigid specifications. What I wanted was a copper-plated finish in the scoring area, with the balance of the head in chrome.

Now it stands to reason that copper plating is much softer than chrome and some new process would have to be evolved. In the average club, the faces are sandblasted. But the MT irons required special treatment. So we came up with what we call our Flame Ceramic Facing Machine, which applies a coating over the facing and gives it not only beautiful color but also increased playability. No one has been able to copy this machine because we have exclusive rights to the process, in which we use ceramic powder, oxygen and hydrogen. Some of our competitors went so far as to try to have it outlawed but we have proved that it meets the most rigid specifications.

Our experimentation with colors in turn resulted in the development of our "Eye-O-Matic" woods. At this time the woods of any manufacturer were set up with one-color fiber faces in the hitting area. We originated two-toning of the faces, for example, in red and black or in red and white. The red "sweet spot," or perfect hitting area, standing forth against the contrasting background, therefore visually set up the "eye" of the golf club and focalized the strength of the hitting area.

We now have undoubtedly one of the most playable facings on any golf club. We refer to it as "impact weight." This facing is made of a special alloy created for us by the Park and Metal Stamping Company of Cincinnati, Ohio.

Some years ago we experimented with a facing made of steel but we couldn't keep the face plate in place no matter what type of screws we used. The face was just too heavy to be held in place against strong hitting.

But this "impact weight" facing we use today is anywhere from one-quarter to one-half ounce heavier than any facing that has ever been put on a wooden club, creating an obviously more effective impact for the hitting area.

These new facings are held in place through the use of the new epoxy glues, which are so strong that the facing would tear the wood off the clubhead before the face would fall out. The need for screws in the facing thus has been virtually eliminated.

Reaching what I consider a new milestone in golf club construction always pleases me deeply and gives me a sense of satisfied accomplishment. Yet no sooner do we start production of a new line of clubs than I begin searching for another improvement. I would have to admit that I am a perfectionist who feels that there is no such thing as perfection. Thus I seek constantly for new fields of progress, new avenues which may lead us to something better. Complacency aggravates me and I must search beyond what is regarded as the absolute best.

As a case in point, I'll refer to the wedge. A number of years ago we developed a utility club which we named the "Double Duty." It was created for the average player to use either in playing pitch shots or for bunker play. This club had a double flange on it with a groove running right through the middle of the flange. The front part was for pitching, which was facilitated through a slight cutting edge. The back was raised a bit higher than the front part of the sole to give it bounce. In playing out of sand the back part would come into play and ease the duffer's job in getting out of sand.

From this we progressed to a club which we named the "Double Service." This one was popularized greatly by Byron Nelson, one of our staff members. Byron, a great player, never carried a sand iron in his bag. His club was this all-purpose weapon and with it he played all kinds of sand shots, bunker shots, pitching shots and approaches from as far out as 115 yards.

This club actually was a weak nine iron with a flange and only six degrees of bounce. A wedge usually carries from 14 to 16 degrees of bounce.

Again, from this club we developed another club which we named the "Double Trouble." This one had a hosel which protruded almost a quarter of an inch in front of the cutting edge on the sole. The purpose of this was to create a position for the average player who knew little of the playability or the manner of playing these trouble clubs. The "Double Trouble," because of the protruding hosel, automatically would put the duffer's hands in the correct position when he addressed the ball and greatly enhanced his chances of getting out of rough or sand.

Claude Harmon, the professional at Winged Foot Golf Club in Mamaroneck, New York, thought this was one of the most playable clubs ever developed and he sold more of them at well-trapped Winged Foot than any other single pro in the country.

I am constantly amazed at the varied sources from which ideas will pop into your head if you are observant.

One afternoon I was sitting in a barber chair and, while getting my hair cut, stared idly out through the plate glass window in front. My eyes finally were attracted to the electric barber pole as its red and white lines spiraled upward inside its glass.

"Hey," I thought to myself, "why not a two-tone grip wound on the club in the same fashion?"

At that time the grips were solid black, brown or red.

When I approached the manufacturers who made leather grips they advised me that it was impossible to use two types of dyes on the one grip. This only made me more determined, so I stripped two grips in half, matching a red half with a black half, sewed them together and, presto, we had a two-tone grip with a barber pole effect.

"It looks like a dago flag," Armour kidded me. "Why don't you get some green into it and finish the job?"

I just laughed at him. Certainly I had the right. Because we worked out the two-color problem and my two-toned grip took the golf world by storm.

As another example, we have a new antique finish available in our woods which developed in my mind one day while I was sunbathing on the beach in front of my home at Jupiter Colony, Florida. Lying there I was fascinated by a breath-taking formation of clouds. Somehow or other they reminded me how, years ago, we burnished shafts to give them a certain attractive coloration. Now the thought occurred to me that we could apply different types of fillers and stains to our woods and create a distinctive antique effect. It developed as another sure-fire eye-appeal product which became a top demand product.

I became intrigued, too, on another occasion, with the fact that our metal furniture at home, being anodized, was able to maintain its coloring and not corrode in the mists off the ocean. Thus I began to search for a way to treat steel shafts so that their color would not fade or tarnish. It was a long and sometimes disheartening trail but we finally perfected this process too.

The result, which soon will be seen on the market, is colored golf shafts for ladies in gold and pastel shades such as blue and lavender.

Our mechanical and technical tests at the factory are never-ending. For instance, a wood head will be exposed to water for about four or five days so that we are able to ascertain its reaction to water. Then, after being taken out of the water, it will be placed in a heating oven for three or four days to fully test both the grade of wood and the finish.

This still isn't enough for me. I expose all of our new clubs to practical tests such as most golfers will put them to unintentionally. I want to see what, under normal conditions, happens to my clubs if they are taken out and played with in the morning dew and then are thrown into the trunk of a car which becomes an oven while sitting in the heat of the parking lot for six or seven hours.

At home I have a tee facing the ocean as well as a sand trap. Every day of the year you'll find all kinds of clubs out there exposed to the ever-changing weather: ocean moisture, rain and blazing heat. When we beat the rust and the cracking of a finish I know we have something of which MacGregor can be proud.

I don't mean this to sound as if I am a cross between Thomas Edison and Albert Einstein. For more than thirty years it has been my good fortune to work shoulder to shoulder in these experiments with a pair of technical geniuses, J. R. (Bob) Lysaght and Clarence Custonborder.

We all three must be perfectly satisfied that a new club will meet completely both our demands and our high standards. Once this has been established, we complete what we call a prototype set and it is presented to our planning committee.

Once accepted and put into production, a new line now comes under the scrutiny of our super sales force, which includes Harold Peterson of Los Angeles, a MacGregor representative for more than forty years, Tom Robbins of the New York metropolitan area and a golf star in his own right, and Harry Adams of Miami, a man who can sell nickels for quarters. This trio, after listening to the presentation of our new line and its qualities, bounces into action with fresh sales ideas and suggestions on how to move in on the custom market.

Speaking of the custom market, Lysaght as head of our custom department handles one of the company's most demanding positions. For the custom department must cater to the idiosyncrasies of people who demand something different from standard or to those who actually need special equipment.

Even in satisfying these specialized demands we feel that we can learn something, and therefore we probe into the reasons why a customer isn't satisfied with our standard line when we feel that we are offering playability personified. Sometimes it is vanity. Other times there are extremely valid reasons.

Your modern-day basketball players, for example, are fellows who range up to seven feet tall and love to play golf. They simply couldn't use an ordinary set of golf clubs because they would be far too short or too light or the grips would not be large enough.

Consider the case of Mike Ditka of the Chicago Bears professional football team. Mike is a big man with medium-length arms and requires a 45-inch driver. The standard clubs would feel like toys to him. Yet, if his arms were shorter, he might need as much as a 49-inch driver.

One of the greatest factors which concerns the custom department is individuality. We have clubs which we call "V.I.P." and which are made to specification as to shafts, grips, swing weight and color of the grips. These are stamped with the owner's name, as are the clubs we make up specially for Perry Como so that he will have a completely personalized set of clubs to fit his station. Quite naturally, Perry is proud of them and we are extremely happy to accommodate him.

If there is one factor this points up it is that we manufacture clubs which run the entire price scale. The custom department handles the super deluxe, extra fancy items which simply won't be found anywhere else because they are specially made for an individual. Our three most famous lines, the Silver Scot, the MT and the DX, adhere rigidly to Professional Golf Association standards and are sold only in pro shops. However, we also are proud of the workmanship and material in our dealer lines and consider them an exceptional buy.

It is always suggested that a person buying clubs should visit a qualified professional. Even if you aren't a member at the club, any pro would be pleased to have you drop into his shop and consult him as to your golfing needs. By watching you hit a few balls, he can select the right clubs.

Yet, in the interests of economy or in getting a good "buy," you need have no fear of visiting sporting goods stores or even most department stores. The salesmen are capable and knowledgeable—sometimes current or former golf pros—and, as I said, we know that our dealer lines are excellent clubs, which gives us a feeling that satisfaction is guaranteed in any price range.

I'm not a salesman and I'm not telling you to get right out there and dig down for MacGregor clubs. But I will tell you two things.

I make them, so forgive my prejudice if I insist that my clubs are the best you can obtain.

And I point pridefully to the fact that my MacGregor clubs have won every championship ever staged, including six Masters championships, five U. S. Open championships and five P.G.A. championships.

Tommy Armour asked me if I would let him say something in this book. Forgive a man his pride but I'm happy to report that the following is what he wrote:

"A small boy had my golf clubs on the first tee and told me he was my caddy. 'Are you big enough to carry those clubs around?' I asked. 'That's easy,' he said, and that was my introduction to Toney Penna.

"That was forty years ago. For many years afterwards, he and I had a very close relationship. He worked for me. Then he went to learn the craftsmanship of club-making under the tutelage of the toughest man in the business, Clarence Rickey, and he learned the art completely.

"His artistry, even at a young age, was very evident by the fact that practically all of the great golfers of the time used his work.

"He then entered the game as a full-fledged professional and, as in everything else he has ever done, he went after it in a very enthusiastic manner. He learned to play golf really well. In fact he was one of the finest players I have ever seen, and that includes everybody. But he had one big failing. He played the easy holes the difficult way, and the difficult holes the easy way. This may sound a trifle ambiguous, but that was his great weakness. Playing straightaway shots was not his dish. It had to be a production. His artistry prevailed, but to his detriment from a scoring standpoint. His name probably will never be in the Hall of Fame as a golfer, but it could easily have been so.

"This type of thinking has prevailed through his whole life: tough, belligerent, kind and generous.

"Then one of the great things that ever happened to MacGregor took place. His joining MacGregor undoubtedly was the greatest stroke of luck that ever happened to the organization because as a club designer he stands alone, and he has many imitators in the field of golf club construction.

"But there is only one Penna. His artistic temperament shows in every piece of merchandise that he produces. It has to be perfect. He is, in fact, quite a man to be just one man."

That's pretty flowery stuff, I'll have to admit. Yet I cherish Tommy's words as an accolade of the highest order because he ranks among the greatest in golf's Hall of Fame.

I entertain no idea of ever making it myself, but I am content because my clubs are there already.

I LEARN THE GAME

You don't have to tell me anything about segregation and the fight for civil rights. When I began to caddy at age eleven or maybe a little bit younger the Scots owned the game of golf. I have always been small of stature, standing no more than five feet, six inches now. But in my boyhood days I was exceptionally small and my first few years in the caddy line were filled with lumps and bruises.

I was born in Naples, Italy, on January 15, 1908, and was brought to the United States by my family when I was five years old. Naturally we were not what you might refer to as Westchester socialites.

As I said, the Scots owned the game of golf and had their favorites among the local boys. Naturally these local boys resented the intrusion of us Italians as well as the Irish and Jewish boys in the area and tried to run us out of the caddy yard.

What it amounted to was several fist fights a day and at times you felt as if you were fighting for your life.

"Hey, dago," was enough to set me after the biggest boy in the yard.

"Guinea" and "wop" were to me like waving a red flag in front of a bull.

I have the greatest respect in the world for one of the finest golf professionals in the country named Herman Barron. As a youngster, fighting the caddy yard battles right along with me, Barron was not very large and not too good with his fists but he took it like a man and fought back every inch of the way to earn acceptance and respect. No one has ever earned my admiration any more than he did, fighting when he had to fight, but, if permitted to go about his work without interference, he did his job quietly and efficiently. Today he is one of the most respected golf professionals in the nation and I consider him a very good friend of mine.

In other words, as far as I am concerned, the word segregation never has had anything to do with the color of a man's skin.

My father had made several trips to the United States before World War I and, settling in Harrison, New York, worked as a carpenter until he earned enough money to bring all of us over.

I have few memories of Italy but I do remember coming over on the ship and scrambling into the first-class section to grab a little better chow than we got in steerage.

We were fortunate that we all were in the United

States when World War I started and it was shortly after the war when I first began to caddy.

We were a tightly-knit family, if not, as I said, Westchester socialites.

My father started his own construction business but unfortunately the crash of 1929 occurred shortly thereafter and he lost just about everything. From that time on we all worked together to keep the family going.

There were six of us, my father and mother, my sister, Fanny, and my two brothers, Nicholas and Charles.

Nick went to college at Columbia University and now is a city engineer in Harrison, New York. He also has his own engineering business. Charlie is the golf professional at the Beverly Country Club in Chicago and I think that Nick at times is a little bit envious when he sees how much fun Charlie and I have had out of golf.

I was small, but strong, when I first began to caddy at the Apawamis Club in Rye, New York. I received thirty-five cents for caddying an eighteen-hole round and in those days it looked like a fortune to me. As I said, it took quite a while to earn acceptance in the caddy yard but eventually everything finally straightened out and I became one of the favorites of George Hughes, the Apawamis caddy master. It was he, more than anyone else, who ended the chaos in the caddy yard by taking the part of us underdogs.

Thus when Hughes became pro at a course across the road called Green Meadows Country Club most of us caddies went right along with him. He was a small, sandy-haired man and it was he who first started me working in the shop, cleaning clubs and getting them out and stowing them away.

Finally the time came when my father, being of the old country school, insisted that I "learn a trade."

"I don't care what trade you learn," my father said, "but it is necessary that everyone learn a trade."

"Will it be all right if I learn the golf trade?" I asked him.

"If that is what you want to do," he said, "it is perfectly all right with me."

As I said, golf was for me so I began to cultivate Bill Moyer, who was the clubmaker and assistant professional at Apawamis. I was young, but I wasn't stupid by any manner or means. One of the first things any Italian family did, no matter where it settled, was to establish a good wine cellar. So I started to snitch a jug of wine from my old man's wine cellar now and then and to take it to Moyer. Maybe it didn't help, but it surely didn't hurt. Because when I asked Moyer for a job in his shop he fortunately had an opening and took me on. I say fortunately because he was, at that time, considered one of the finest clubmakers in the world.

Merely watching Moyer at work was an education. Of course in those days all clubs had hickory shafts. Bill would pick out a hickory shaft for, let's say, a two-iron and smell the wood. Why he did this I'll never know but it certainly must have told him something. He would then fit into the hosel of the iron and then meticulously straighten the shaft, sand it down, rub pitch into the grain of the shaft, let it stand, wet it, apply more pitch for more firmness so that the grain would be filled with pitch and shellac to make it as impervious as possible to the weather.

Watching Moyer was watching an artist at work. Wooden heads, for example, were shaped out of six-inch blocks of persimmon. This persimmon, incidentally, comes from only one place in the country, which is Memphis, Tennessee. We would get the persimmon in six-inch blocks, cut them in L-shaped fashion and have two potential heads out of each block. From there you started whittling with rasp and file until you had something that looked like the head of a golf club. These blocks then were half-seasoned. They were set aside to dry again. Moyer worked out a scheme of drying them in the boiler room, right there in the clubhouse.

The head professional at Apawamis at that time was a man by the name of Billy Potts, a short, stocky man who could knock the ball a country mile. One of my most vivid memories of that time was watching Potts stand on the first tee at Apawamis and try to drive the green of the first hole, a shot of three hundred and sixty-five yards.

This hole is a very famous one in the history of golf. It was on this hole in 1911 that the first foreigner ever won the National Amateur Golf Championship. His name was Harold Hilton and he defeated Fred Herreshoff on the first extra hole in a playoff.

Herreshoff was on the green in regulation figures putting for a birdie and Hilton hadn't even played his second shot. It looked as if it was all over for him because he practically shanked his second shot far to the right of the green. But the ball hit a rock and bounced about eight feet from the hole. Taking advantage of this break he holed the putt for a birdie three to beat Herreshoff.

As a young boy I had a great deal of difficulty understanding the extremely high social barriers between various classes. My father always talked of the great opportunities for the foreign-born in the United States and yet Potts, the head professional at Apawamis, while a fine gentleman with good manners and a man who was always beautifully dressed, wasn't allowed in the clubhouse. He ate in the chauffeurs' quarters.

In those days, of course, golf had not attained the stature which it enjoys in this era. People paid a great deal of money to belong to a country club which actually was a spot in which the socialites gathered. You were a so-called blueblood or you weren't. The distinction was finely drawn and rigidly held to.

The changes which I witnessed over the years are extremely fascinating to me. Now the courses and the clubs are wide open to the golf professional. As a matter of fact the first thing a club does is to look for a professional with a "name" who will enhance the reputation of the club. This is a direct result of the manner in which the game has changed, and with it the social distinctions.

Tommy Armour, Coral Gables, Florida, 1935 (Wide World)

There was a time, for example, when an amateur teeing off in a major championship was referred to by the announcer as "Mister" Bobby Jones. The pro was simply Toney Penna: no "Mister."

But the fantastic growth of the game has altered all this over the last few years. With the explosion of the game of golf the top tournament players, both amateur and professional, started to become household names. Rapidly the barriers that had existed so long began to crumble, dissolving like so much sand under the waves of publicity and acclaim.

Today the professionals are not only privileged guests in the clubhouse but are also welcomed with open arms in the most socially prominent homes.

There are any number of reasons for this metamorphosis. In the old days, it possibly is quite true, all of the graduates of the caddy ranks were not what you might refer to as polished gentlemen. But most of your professionals today are college products who have become celebrities as much sought after as any stars of the entertainment world.

Another factor is what might be referred to as the great real estate gimmick. This is a case in which a syndicate of wealthy men buys a large tract of land. The gimmick is that they build a beautiful golf course and plush clubhouse as a lure to attract customers who will construct high-priced homes around and frequently on the golf course. As an aid, and a large one, in obtaining publicity for their project the first thing that they do is to obtain the services of a professional with a nationally known name. This enhances both the reputation of the club and the salability of the real estate.

The social barrier was a carry-over from the game as it was born and weaned in the British Isles. Walter Hagen made the first dent in this almost visible fence when, barred from the clubhouse during a tournament in Britain, he drove up in a Rolls-Royce and proceeded to change his shoes in front of all who cared to watch. How classy can you get?

This invisible wall still exists in most foreign countries but, as I have pointed out, it is practically nonexistent in the United States today.

The wall began to dissolve in this country when players such as Gene Sarazen, Walter Hagen, Tommy Armour and Johnny Farrell, and many others who were building national reputations with their golf clubs, were invited into the mansions of the mighty and proved themselves to be gentlemen as well as golfers. In many cases they proved themselves to their hosts as better guests than some of their socially prominent friends. For these champions of the fairway all were delightfully entertaining. On the other hand, society has always had its boors who never earned their fortunes but inherited them and if the truth be known probably couldn't have sold quarters for nickels.

Thus it was that these earlier champions started the trend which the boys of today have followed through so flawlessly, so that your professional golfer today stands on equal footing with society's finest.

I had worked for Moyer a little over a year at Apawamis, when Alex Smith became the head professional at Westchester Country Club and I heard that he was looking for someone to work in his shop.

Westchester probably is one of the finest clubs ever built. It had two eighteen-hole courses plus a nine-hole pitch and putt course, polo fields, driveways running through the property and homes of $50,000 and more. The clubhouse with some three hundred rooms was magnificent.

However, I had worked into a very smooth routine working for Moyer and before I contemplated giving up my job with him I went over to Westchester to size up the situation.

I arrived there late one afternoon and the caddy master was standing in the doorway of the shop holding a big leather bag.

"Do you need a caddy?" I asked him.

He nodded his head vigorously.

"Sure," he said. "Go on and take it, it's okay."

I shouldered the bag and began the walk of about a hundred and fifty yards from the caddy house to the south course. Halfway there my path was blocked by a strapping six-footer whose name, I learned later, was Sonny Gordon, a basketball player of some note.

"Hand it over," he said, reaching for the bag. "This is my steady man and this is my bag."

I was five feet, two inches tall and weighed about a hundred and ten pounds, but I long since had learned how to fight my way around the caddy yard and I wasn't about to give up the bag.

"Over my dead body," I snapped at him.

Once more he grabbed at the bag and with this, I took out a club, held it like a baseball bat and left no doubt in his mind that I was going to clout him right over the head.

"The caddy master gave me this bag and I'm going to carry it," I told him. "If you try to take it you're going to be wearing this club in your skull."

He backed off and that day I started to caddy regularly for Tommy Armour.

Meanwhile, I decided to take the job in Alex Smith's golf shop. I worked with a man named Stanley "Stitchy" Bernard and between us we shined and took care of five hundred sets of clubs every day.

This still ranks in my mind as one of the smartest moves I ever made, because Alex Smith was completely wonderful to me. I still had a slight Italian accent and Alex talked to me like a father, advising me to quit fighting the world when I was called names and to help myself by learning how to talk properly, build up a better vocabulary and train myself to have poise and polish.

I worked eight hours a day in the shop, making and repairing clubs, and Alex was always quick to teach me the niceties. Then, after a while, he would arrange a golf game for me in the evenings, usually with the members. These were high-class men, industrial and social leaders, and with his recommendation they accepted me readily.

"Watch how they talk and how they act," he told me.

I stayed there two years and began a solid friendship with Armour, who at that time was golfing secretary of the club.

Then came a day when Armour told me that he was taking the head professional job at the Congressional Country Club in Washington, where Ken Venturi won the United States Open Golf Championship in 1964. Armour admittedly knew little and cared less about operating a shop. What he was interested in was playing and teaching. I was only seventeen years old at the time but he took me with him as his assistant to run the shop and also to teach at times. It worked out very well for a couple of years but then Tommy won the United States Open in 1927 in a playoff against "Lighthorse Harry" Cooper at Oakmont. Tommy won the championship by tying Cooper on the final hole with a fine iron shot. He made the shot with a mongrel iron which he could use as a two-, a three- or a four-iron merely by opening or closing the blade.

It was here that the late Grantland Rice, one of the world's finest sportswriters, made Tommy famous as the "Iron Master."

Armour became very much in demand following his victory in the U. S. Open and subsequently went to the Tam O' Shanter Club in Detroit. I returned to New York and began working as a clubmaker for Jimmy

Donaldson at Fenimore Country Club. This now is known as Fenway Country Club and Herman Barron, my old friend of the caddying days, is the head professional there. However, it was while I was at Fenimore that I became acquainted with the late Leo Diegel as well as with "Wild Bill" Mehlhorn.

Mehlhorn played a tremendously vital role in my life when he took a job as head professional of a club in Pensacola, Florida. For I went with him as his chief assistant. Bill wasn't too enchanted with running a club, preferring to play tournament golf, so I wound up running the club. It wasn't too long before he told me he was leaving his job and so at twenty-two I was given the job as head pro of the Osceola Golf Club, owned by the City of Pensacola. The job paid me two hundred dollars a month as head pro plus all I could make on the side in the way of lessons and shop sales.

Now that I was running my own show I had time to play occasionally in tournaments too and I felt I was a big man when I went out and won the Southeastern Open Championship. One of the friends I made at the Pensacola club was a man named Dick Merritt, who was the county solicitor.

We played golf together a great deal and one day I went to his office to pick him up. I was bowled over completely by his secretary, a tiny blonde named Angela Clark. Dick told me that he was married to her sister and that Angela was engaged to be married.

It took me some time to get up nerve enough to ask

her for a date. After all, she was from an old Southern family and Toney Penna was just an ex-caddy still fighting a slight Italian accent.

She finally agreed to have a date with me and that was the end of her other engagement. Two months later we were married. So it was that at twenty-five I happily became a father. We had our first son, Anthony Geraldo Penna, Jr. We call him Gerry and have from the start because I wasn't about to have two Toneys around the house.

Gerry graduated from Florida State as a major in mathematics and currently works for Pratt-Whitney. Our second child, Tom, was born five years later. He was an honor student in math at Georgia Tech and works for General Electric. Later on we had a daughter, Claire, who is married and residing in Lansing, Michigan, and who has made Toney Penna a two-time grandfather.

While I was head pro at the Osceola Golf Club, many officers would play at the club who were stationed at the Pensacola Naval Air Station. One of these was a captain who later gained fame as Admiral "Bull" Halsey. He was a great golf bug/buff and we became very friendly. Thus it was that Angela and I would be invited to attend dances at the Naval Air Station.

All my life we had had Chianti on the table at meals. I never drank milk, and don't now. However, it was only on special occasions that I would drink a highball.

So it didn't take too much to loosen my tongue at both ends one night when we went to a dance at the

Naval Air Station and Halsey, who was taking flight training, promoted a discussion as to whether it took more intestinal fortitude to drop a six-foot putt with a lot of money on the line or to jump out of an airplane with a parachute. As I said, I had had a couple of drinks and I felt exceptionally valorous.

"How could it take any guts to jump out of an airplane?" I asked. "All you have to do is jump and pull the ring."

Halsey asked me whether I would jump.

"Of course I'd jump," I said.

Several of the other officers at the table insisted that I wouldn't have the nerve and before I knew it everybody was betting either that I would, or that I wouldn't.

As I said, that bottled stuff had made me real brave. I even bet twenty-five dollars that I would.

We went home and I forgot all about it. But the next morning at 8 A.M. there was a knock on the door and outside stood a naval lieutenant.

"Come on," he told me. "We're waiting for you at the emergency landing field near the golf course."

Halsey had set it up so that the lieutenant was to land near the course, leave the student he was flying at the emergency field, and take me up for my jump.

"Wait a minute! Wait a minute!" I snorted. "This thing is all a gag."

The lieutenant shook his head sternly.

"Captain Halsey doesn't give me the impression it's a joke," the lieutenant said. "I'm to deliver you and you're going with me."

What could I do? Feeling watery in the knees I got in the car with him and figured that possibly I might be able to talk them all out of it when we reached the emergency landing field.

But at the field there was only this open cockpit plane, and the wide-eyed student. Before I knew it the lieutenant had strapped me into a parachute and boosted me into the plane. I had hardly gulped my Adam's apple back down out of my mouth when we were off and up. Looking around I could see an unusually large number of planes circling above us. It was the betters of the previous evening flying around like vultures and waiting to see what would happen to Toney Penna.

"Are you ready?" the lieutenant shouted to me.

"No, sir." I shook my head. "Just get me down out of this thing."

He pointed at the planes above.

"Look," he said. "They are all watching you."

There was no way, I figured, that they were going to get Toney to jump out of this thing.

"Stand up."

I shook my head again. "Nothing doing."

"Stand up," the lieutenant ordered again.

Weakly, as if hypnotized, I stood up gingerly. The next thing I knew the lieutenant had flipped the ship over and I was dumped out before I could even try to grab hold of some part of the airplane.

"Count to ten," I heard him shout just before he flipped me loose.

Nobody ever pulled the ripcord quicker than I did. Then for a few moments it didn't seem so bad floating through the air.

But all of a sudden the ground was racing up to grab me.

I must have made the worst parachute landing in the history of aviation. When I landed I broke my ankle, bruised both knees, scraped both elbows and had my clothes virtually torn off me.

Let me just say in conclusion to this escapade that I'd take the six-foot putt anytime and for any amount of money.

Life at Pensacola was pleasant but became increasingly dull to me. I played a tremendous amount of golf and really had my game in top shape but I began to feel as if I was buried in the backwater of some bayou. I kept telling myself that if I ever was going to get anywhere in the game of golf I would have to leave Pensacola. While I did not discuss this with anyone, it all came to a head for me one afternoon when I went to City Hall and had an argument with the City Manager, who technically was my boss.

"Take your job and stick someone else with it," I said, turning and leaving the City Manager's office, slamming the door behind me in solid punctuation of my decision.

My old friend Tommy Armour at this time was at Boca Raton, on the Atlantic side of Florida. I decided that I would go to him for advice. He thoroughly understood my dissatisfaction with being buried in Pensacola and my feeling that I was in a rut. So he invited me to stay with him for a while and, as we played a few games of golf, Tommy was visibly surprised at the manner in which my golf game had improved.

Then came the morning when I played a round on Boca Raton's south course, one no longer in existence but at that time considered one of the finest in the country, along with Bobby Cruickshank and Tommy Taylor. I shot a 67 and when we all gathered around Armour's famed Round Table for lunch all Cruickshank talked about was what he called my "unbelievable" round, detailing it shot by shot. Finally Armour jumped up and said to me:

"What the hell are you doing sitting around here? They're playing a five-thousand-dollar tournament down at Hollywood. Get your tail down there and take a crack at it."

"Let's go," prodded Cruickshank, and I didn't need much encouragement. Maybe five thousand dollars doesn't sound like a great deal of money in these days of one-hundred-thousand-dollar purses but in those days it was a heap of money.

Within a few minutes we had jumped into Bobby's car and were heading for Hollywood, which is only a few miles north of Miami. On our arrival, we paid our entry fee right on the first tee, and they teed us off with Helen Hicks, one of the early women professionals.

Strangely enough, when I teed it up in the Hollywood Open I was not the least bit nervous. I felt that this was my element completely and that, untested and untried, I still belonged in this company.

Clarence Rickey, the MacGregor man responsible for Toney Penna's career in golf club artistry (MacGregor)

However, I was quite a bit surprised when I shot a sixty-four, the lowest round of my career to that point, and at the end of that opening round found myself leading the field by three strokes. Cruickshank and Vic Ghezzi were tied for second place with sixty-sevens.

No, I am sorry to report, I did not win the tournament. I came up to the last hole needing a long putt to beat Ghezzi for first-place money. I putted boldly for the cup and missed, sliding on past. Then, needing that putt to tie for the lead and force a playoff, I missed coming back. So it was that taking three putts to get down on the final hole cost me the tournament by a stroke.

Yet this did convince me that I could play tournament golf with the best of them. Of course I felt I had previously proved this to myself my winning the Southeastern P.G.A. in 1933. But, despite my cockiness, I would have to admit in looking back that I had a tremendous lot going against me in those days.

Temperament plays a vast part in the makeup of a winning tournament golfer and I confess that I had a blazing Latin temperament with which to cope. I would get so furious with myself when I made a mistake, choosing the wrong club or playing the wrong type of shot, that I would blow sky-high and it would cost me three or four more shots before I could settle down again.

Tournament golf in those days was not the week in, week out gold-dust trail that it is today. Tournaments were well scattered and the ideal setup was to have a club job, which demanded most of your time. If you played in a half-dozen tournaments a year, you were really on the "circuit."

So, following my major debut in the Hollywood Open, I headed on back to Boca Raton to spend a little more time with Armour. Tommy, of course, was a national figure in golf in those days and Boca Raton was one of the plush citadels of golf. This proved fortunate for me because there I was introduced to Ray Franzen, owner of the Itasca Country Club in Itasca, Illinois. We played golf together and became friends rapidly. I was flattered when he offered me the job as head professional at Itasca, a beautiful golf course which actually was the first fine golf job of my entire life.

Gathering up my family I headed for Illinois and settled quickly and happily into my new position as head pro at Itasca.

I had been there some time when I received a visitor named Clarence Rickey who was to make a tremendous and lasting impression on my life. Rickey was president and general manager of MacGregor, known then as Crawford, MacGregor, and Canby Company. It had been a firm involved in shoe-last manufacturing and Rickey had put them into the golf club business. He had started with Tommy Armour as the chief name on his professional golf club line.

Mr. Rickey made a practice of calling on professionals at various golf courses and it was in this manner, when he stopped at Itasca, that I met him. He was a short, stout, cheerful man who was noted as a great salesman. And the time came when he really sold me a bill of goods.

For one day, during another of his visits, he said to me:

"Toney, you have something that I can use in my business."

I was puzzled. "What's that?"

"You have a fine, sunny personality," he said, "and you would make a wonderful emissary for MacGregor. You are going to come to work for me."

I looked at him startled and wide-eyed. I was completely happy with my job at Itasca and had no intention whatsoever of leaving.

"You must be out of your mind." I laughed at him. "I have a fine job, a good salary and my home is here. I am doing exceptionally well. If you think I'm going to leave this, Mr. Rickey, you have got another guess coming."

As I said, Mr. Rickey was a salesman.

He kept coming back, always pressuring me to go to work for him, and in 1934 almost before I knew it I found myself working as an "emissary" for Clarence Rickey and MacGregor.

I didn't realize it at the time, but, as I said, it was one of the greatest breaks of my life.

For this was the start of a career which, at this writing, has extended over thirty-one wonderful years. I became a staff member for MacGregor at five hundred dollars a month and within six months Mr. Rickey had given me the first of many raises which I have received. And in all this time I have never once had a contract with this company.

It was Rickey's plan that I should play in as many tournaments as possible, traveling across the country and visiting as often as possible with the professionals at the various country clubs, checking on our sales and our equipment and attempting to find out from these professionals how we could improve our equipment.

Playing in tournaments was easy because, as I have said, there was not a tournament every week as there is in the current era. The professional of those times had only twelve or fifteen tournaments a year in which to compete. The rest of the time he was expected to remain at home and take care of his job. Thus most of the professionals were able to compete in only about half of the tournaments listed.

The winter circuit at that time consisted of the Los Angeles Open, the San Francisco Match Play, San Diego, Caliente and San Antonio. After this there was a general dissembling to the home ports. Here the pro was expected to take over getting his club ready for spring and summer play and making sure that all the equipment that had been stowed away through the period of ice and snow was ready for the club members.

Thus the U. S. Open Golf Championship in June would be about the first one which followed the brief winter tour.

It was a very difficult job that I had assumed. Rickey

had impressed upon me the necessity of making personal appearances at every club in any and every area in which I traveled. Therefore when I hit the winter tour, I would tee off a great many times without a single practice round. The reason was that in visiting clubs in the neighborhood it seemed politic for me to play a round with the home pro rather than worry about getting ready for the local tournament. So the best that I was able to accomplish in the year 1936 was runner-up in the Cotton States Open.

I still remember with a chuckle the first order I received for a set of golf clubs while visiting one of these clubs in doing my missionary work. I was so excited that I phoned the order in to Mr. Rickey, and there went the profit on that set right down the drain.

At the 1937 Los Angeles Open I met Willie Goggin and Jimmy Demaret, and we immediately became great friends. In no time at all we were referred to by the other pros as the "gruesome threesome." For the three of us teamed up and decided to travel from tournament to tournament by car. This was economical and we were able to share the driving chores.

By this time I was really "contact happy." I did not go into any section without immediately visiting all of the clubs in the area and striking up a friendship with the local professionals. Goggin and Demaret went along with me as often as possible and were a great help in my missionary work. We played not only with the local professionals at their clubs but also with their members. It was in this manner that we met such men as

Del Webb and Dan Topping, later to become co-owners of the New York Yankees baseball team. Back then we also played golf with Barry Goldwater at Phoenix. He may have been defeated in the 1964 presidential election but he was a real tough man to handle on the golf course and made you play your heart out because if you didn't, he'd beat out your brains for a twenty-dollar Nassau.

We three, Goggin, Demaret and I, had great times together. I remember with great gusto the time Jimmy was delayed in San Francisco and caused us to drive all night to get to Phoenix the next day. They called me the "madman" because I liked to drive fast. Going across the desert, with no traffic policemen hiding behind every bush, I could really let fly. Of course our car was loaded with clothing, golf bags and golf clubs. Jimmy and Willie were sound asleep in the back and I was doing better than one hundred miles an hour when Demaret sat up with a yelp.

"Stop the car, for the love of Pete," Demaret howled. "You are going to kill all of us."

I let the car idle to a halt, got out and stretched wearily.

"Okay," I told him, "you take over because I am kind of tired myself."

I don't know what awakened me but I sat up in the back seat and could hardly believe my eyes.

Demaret was driving through the desert at a cool one hundred and ten miles an hour without any lights on.

"Just what in the devil are you doing driving without any lights on?" I demanded excitedly.

"Look, we got lots of moonlight," Jimmy replied. "All I'm trying to do, old buddy, is to save the battery."

We had good times here and there, but actually we were doing our share of winning a few dollars here and a few dollars there. Personally, I had to win. I had to send money home to the family. On top of this, I have always traveled top drawer. I am not one of those fellows who will tell you that he ate oranges out of an orange grove to keep from starving. Or that he ate at hamburger stands or lived on doughnuts and coffee. I didn't. Wherever we went we had room service, we ate the best and we wore the best clothes possible. There are times I remember when we had to be chased with the bill but I always figured that first class was the best way to impress people.

I loved big, powerful automobiles and I loved fancy clothes. Anytime I saw something different in clothing, even if I didn't have the money to buy it, I had to have it. This was particularly so if it was different from what everybody else was wearing out on the golf course.

For example, I was having my shoes handmade in New York City at eighty-five dollars a pair. Now, let's face it, I was a long way from being able to afford this kind of fancy footwear.

But I managed handsomely. The place where I bought these shoes had Italian shoemakers or bootmakers who worked in the back of the shop. I didn't have the cash.

But all I had to do was smuggle in a couple of gallons of my father's dago red and they made me all the shoes I wanted. No cash.

It was the same way with automobiles. Anytime a new car came out and appealed to me, I had to have it. At this time, Mr. Rickey was furnishing me with a company car. There were times when the car was only two or three months old and I would spot a new model car which had just appeared on the market. I had to have it. And if they said it was the fastest thing on the road there was no possible way to keep me out of the driver's seat.

One of the first of the really fast automobiles that I had was a Buick Century, then one of the fastest automobiles on the market. I left the New Orleans Open en route to Pensacola, Florida, which was where the next tournament was to be played and was really rolling down Route 90 from New Orleans to Pensacola. I was clocking off about ninety miles an hour and all of a sudden there was a police car right behind me. I was certain that this police car couldn't catch me if I could keep the open road in front of me. I was a dead duck if anybody got in my way and I had to slow down.

My car was really ticking it over. He couldn't gain an inch on me but he stayed right there in my rear-view mirror as the miles fled behind us. He had the siren wailing and I knew that if he ever caught me I wasn't going to be in the jail but under the jail.

Suddenly a car loomed in front of me and as I hurtled

by I saw that it was being driven by Henry Picard. In a few minutes I passed another car which contained Dutch Harrison and Bob Hamilton.

Hamilton told me later that he leaned over to Harrison and said: "There goes Penna, the wild man."

And a minute behind me the police car zoomed past them too.

All of a sudden the police car disappeared from sight behind me but I still kept flying down the road to Pensacola.

Hamilton told me that they had traveled only a few miles after I passed them when they came up to the police car standing on the side of the road, steam pouring out of the radiator, the policeman standing there staring at it—and no Penna in sight.

Penna, by that time, was in Pensacola.

I hate to admit it, but even today I have difficulty controlling those horses.

As a matter of fact, it's been only two or three years since a state highway patrolman came to my house in Jupiter, Florida, and rang the bell.

"Mr. Penna," he said, "I'm awfully sorry but I'm here on official business. We have to pick up your license. You've had too many speed tickets over the last few months and your license is revoked until further notice."

I had to take another driver's examination before I finally got back my license.

When I came off the tour that spring of 1937 I immediately headed back to the MacGregor plant and Mr. Rickey and I held a number of detailed conferences

Toney Penna, Bob Lysaugh, Clarence Custonborder at the MacGregor milling machine (MacGregor)

on just what we should do about improving our sales. I told him that from all my contacts made while on the road the home club professionals wherever I had done my missionary work were in complete accord with the company and its policy of winning friends but that everywhere they had insisted that we must make various improvements in our merchandise.

The first thing I suggested was that we make some exceptionally fine wooden clubs. MacGregor at that time had as its chief club designer a man named Willie Sime. He was noted as the inventor of a club called the bap, and it was one of the most popular wooden clubs that ever had been made, but no matter what suggestions were given to Sime regarding the shaping of new types of wooden clubs, whatever he producd always came out looking exactly like the old bap. I insisted that we had to make substantially different models of wooden clubs to attract the trade. Sime wouldn't budge an inch.

"The bap has been good enough for MacGregor for ten years or more and it's good enough right now," he argued.

I insisted, on the other hand, that we were entering an era where ever-increasing play and merchandising demanded that we experiment and produce increasingly attractive designs. As I have said, I have a hot Latin temper and the argument grew to magnificent proportions. It was a straight-out showdown and Mr. Rickey stood by me.

Sime, outraged at being overruled in favor of what

he termed a "Johnny-come-lately," resigned from the company.

In the final analysis, of course, this simply meant more duties for me.

Almost before I knew what was happening, I was spending more time in the plant than almost anyone else. I found a ready ally in a man by the name of Clarence Custonborder and we worked together steadily, attempting to produce a variety of new-type woods. "Cuzzy" and I also began to attempt to modify some of our irons. We threw out all the rules and began from scratch. I hammered home the point that eye appeal was as important as playability, and "Cuzzy" went along with me.

My feeling was, and always has been, that eye appeal is what helped to make the automobile industry as large as it is. Most women when they go in to buy an automobile don't care at all what is under the hood. First of all they have to like the lines of the car and then, naturally, it comes down to a question of which colors please them.

So it was that I insisted on putting eye appeal into the golf club, and I believe that this was my first real contribution to the manufacturing industry. I had observed that not only women but also men had to like the look of the clubs they purchased.

Thus since 1936 three letters have been my Bible: O.R.C.—observing, remembering and comparing.

Rickey was way ahead of me. He knew that tournament golf was in my blood and that I thought I could play with the best of them. As I look back, I realize that he wanted me in the plant full-time, but when I wasn't there he did not worry too much about my playing in tournaments. When I was on the road, it was his theory, I would spend much of my time making friends for MacGregor and selling the company to the professionals with whom I associated.

If he had insisted that I stay at the plant I am quite certain that I would have chucked the whole tournament business. But he realized I was not quite ready, at that time, to make the complete transition. So it was that he soft-soaped me into believing I could do both jobs.

"There are only ten or twelve tournaments that you want to play in every year," he said. "I am certain you can do both. Go ahead. Try to keep your name up there in the headlines because it opens doors for us which would be closed if you weren't playing."

It was a real con job.

I did pull a fast one on him by getting him to agree that whenever I played in a tournament I would not have to be bothered with duties at the factory or selling. So for a while I concentrated on my golf and worked religiously on my game.

Putting the factory out of my mind for a time I finally hit the golfing jackpot with my first victory. This was the Pennsylvania Open at Merion Country Club that summer of 1937 and I won it against a field which included such fine players as Jimmy Demaret, Willie

Goggin, "Wild Bill" Mehlhorn, "Lighthorse Harry" Cooper, and a number of others.

Merion is ranked as one of the finest golf courses in the entire nation and despite the fact that we played one round in the rain I compiled a 289 which was the first time that 290 had been broken over that course.

I was fortunate enough to finish third in the summer of 1938 in the National Open at Cherry Hill in Denver, Colorado. The Master's Tournament, which since then has become one of the most famous events in the golfing world, had been started in 1934. As a result of finishing third in the U. S. Open at Cherry Hill I qualified for my first Masters in 1938.

Teeing off in the Masters in the spring of 1939 was one of the greatest thrills of my life. The golf course is one of the most beautiful in the world and I must rate the tournament itself as the very best. One of the proudest facets of my career is that I played in the Masters from 1938 until 1953. I am sorry to say that I never won it. My best finish was a tie for eighth in 1947, the year it was captured by my old buddy Demaret. However, I did finish in the top ten three times and in the top twenty seven times.

Even now, going back there merely as a spectator every year still gives me a tremendous thrill.

In 1938 I won what was then considered one of the major events on the tour when I came home first in the Kansas City Open. That year, also, I was chosen one of the All-American golf team, but being foreign-born I could not be named to the Ryder Cup team as a player for the United States.

I do not necessarily argue with this rule in connection with selecting the Ryder Cup team but I do feel that something should be done about the rule that a player must be a professional for five years before he can be named to the team.

It seems somewhat ludicrous to me that players such as Jack Nicklaus and Bobby Nichols are ineligible to play for the United States on the Ryder Cup Team. Nicklaus, in less than four years as a professional, won the Masters twice, the United States Open and the P.G.A. Championship. Nichols was ineligible for the same reason, although he too had won the P.G.A. Championship. It doesn't make a great deal of sense to me that these two champions of their profession should be kept out of action and stripped of this honor merely because they have not been professionals for five years.

Before this rule was instituted, Sammy Snead played on the Ryder Cup team in his second year as a professional. After the rule was instituted, Lawson Little, one of the truly great match players in the history of golf, was ineligible, as was Cary Middlecoff.

Each year my job with MacGregor was becoming more demanding and, at the same time, tournament golf was growing fantastically. But I struggled along trying to carry water on both shoulders and I am certain that this kept me from being a more frequent winner on the tournament trail.

One of the richest moments of my competitive career, as far as I am concerned, came when I tied Demaret at Houston for the Western Open.

This was Jimmy's hometown and it being the first time that a Texan had a chance to win a major title under those circumstances there were five thousand fans out there rooting for Jimmy and I might as well have been playing on the moon. I do not say this as an excuse for the fact that Demaret knocked me off with a very fine score. But I am quite certain that if I had defeated him at River Oaks that afternoon I would have been ridden out of town on a rail.

Jimmy loved it. The crowd thought it was fantastic. Penna was delighted to settle for second-place money.

It is amazing how the years fly by. I kept getting my piece of the tournament prize money here and there and the years ran one into another rapidly, their speed increased by the fact that I was handling two jobs. There was the tournament season and there were those increasingly frequent trips to the MacGregor factory.

I did win the Atlanta Open in 1947 and I must consider it one of the highlights of my career because this was the home of the immortal Bobby Jones and the "Emperor" was in the gallery. It was one of my better years because I was runner-up in the Colonial Invitation as well as the Los Angeles Open, and also tied for eighth in the Masters.

My greatest triumph came in 1948, when I captured the North-South Open, played over one of the finest courses in the world—number two course at Pinehurst. I won it with a score of 285 and Sammy Snead came home second behind me.

One of those who finished back of me in the field that day was a young amateur named Julius Boros. Through the years, Boros has established himself as one of the finest golfers and gentlemen in the game. I did try to sign him as a member of our MacGregor staff but, unfortunately, he decided to cast his lot with another company.

It seems impossible that the years in which I could play golf all day and night rode by so swiftly and yet the time came when I knew, as if someone had turned on a spotlight in my skull, that I would have to devote all my energies to my job with MacGregor. Combining the two jobs, playing golf and visiting all the club professionals possible, just became too much work and I had to concede that I could not do both of them. Mr. Rickey smiled when I told him of my decision.

"It's been a long time coming, Toney," he told me, "but I knew that eventually you would see the light."

"Yes," I agreed. "And I know now that you finally have got what you have been driving for these last few years."

It still, even today, is great fun to tee it up in a local tournament. The "old man" still can shoot a pretty hot stick. But finally I have settled into the niche Rickey reserved for me so long ago.

GUSTY MEMORIES

In looking back over my career in golf, both as a player and as a club designer, the laughs are too many to remember and some too racy to relate.

Yet one which stands out vividly in my memory concerned my first effort to sign up a staff member, what is known as an advisory staff member, whose duties would be to play the tour as a representative of the MacGregor Company, do missionary work along the same lines as I was doing, and advise us on how we could make better golf clubs.

The first player I thought of signing up for MacGregor was Jimmy Demaret. Jimmy was one of the finest, brightest, most colorful personalities in the game, and still is. I knew that he was a fine player who was going to make a lasting mark on the game. This has long since been proved and I need merely to point to the fact that he was the first man to win the Masters Championship three times.

I wanted Jimmy working on our side and I suggested his name to Mr. Rickey.

So, during the 1937 United States Open Championship at Oakland Hills Country Club in Birmingham, Michigan, I introduced Demaret to Rickey and after Jimmy had left I told Mr. Rickey that I would like to sign Jimmy as one of our staff members. Mr. Rickey looked at me speculatively and then said:

"Now wait just a minute, Toney. If I understand you correctly, this Demaret is from Houston, Texas. Now who in the world plays golf in Texas? Let's get some of these boys affiliated with our company who are from larger metropolitan areas so that we can get some of that mass business and sell a greater percentage of golf clubs."

I might interject here that every company which produces golf equipment in these days has a large staff of these advisory members. They not only have their company's name printed in large letters on their golf bags, like walking signboards, but they also do a great deal of missionary and good-will work.

In those early days we would sign a good player for five hundred dollars and the company would match the purse they earned in winning one of the major tournaments.

I protested to Mr. Rickey that Demaret would be well worth the investment because of his dash, color and outgoing personality.

Rickey couldn't see it my way. "I still think you can spend five hundred dollars a lot more usefully than that," he told me.

However, I had arranged to take Jimmy to dinner with us at a night spot where Wayne King, one of the leading orchestra leaders of the day, was playing at the dinner show.

Jimmy knew Wayne King and while we were having dinner the orchestra leader asked Demaret, with quite a vocal build-up, to come to the bandstand and sing a number with him.

There is no question in my mind but what Demaret could have been one of the most renowned singers in the country. He had a fine voice, à la Bing Crosby, and he could croon with the best of them.

Jimmy went to the bandstand and my laughing friend from Texas was a sensation.

Mr. Rickey watched him, wide-eyed, and before Jimmy had finished singing he turned around to me, nodding vigorously.

"Toney, I don't know whether this boy can play golf or not, that's your department, but as far as a good-will ambassador is concerned, sign him up because he's worth every penny of it. He sure has what it takes and all the personality that I'm looking for, because I think that's just as important in selling golf clubs as it is to be able to play with them."

It's typical of the irrespressible Demaret how he repaid me, in spades, for signing him up with MacGregor.

I have always been blessed with exceedingly white

and even teeth. One day shortly thereafter we were in a locker room when a man who was connected with an agency that handled a toothpaste account asked me whether I would like to endorse their product.

"You'd better be careful about this guy," Jimmy said with a straight face. "He has teeth but he washes them with Sani-Flush."

"You mean he doesn't use toothpaste?" The man frowned.

"Toothpaste!" Jimmy snorted. "I told you he doesn't even know what toothpaste is."

Jimmy rose abruptly and left the room and I could see his shoulders shaking he was laughing so hard.

The man kept staring at me and finally, indecision written all over his face, he asked: "Are those teeth really yours?"

By this time the old Penna temper was beginning to go through the top of the thermometer.

"Of course they're real, you dope," I told him.

He looked at me silently a few more minutes and then he said: "Would you mind if I felt them?"

By this time I had just about had all of this nonsense I was going to take but, vanity being vanity, I opened my mouth and said, "Go ahead and feel for yourself."

The guy actually reached up and tugged on my front teeth. Then, shaking his head, he stood up and said:

"It's just too bad you don't use toothpaste. But, after all, those teeth do look false anyhow."

With that he walked away leaving me sitting there with my mouth still open.

Because of my explosive temper I always was a great butt for practical jokes by Demaret, Goggin and another fellow named Tommy LoPresti, who joined us occasionally on the tour. LoPresti, who was voted Golfer of the Year by the Professional Golf Association a couple of years ago, was a great practical joker.

I recall, with amusement now, although at the time I was ready to kill all three of them, another occasion when we were playing in the Biltmore Open in Miami.

Goggin and LoPresti had a room adjoining one occupied by Demaret and me. We had a connecting door and it was a pleasant setup.

On this particular afternoon I had just taken a bath when there was a knock on the door. I had a towel in my hand and I held it draped loosely around me while I cautiously opened the door and peered out. There stood Demaret.

"Why don't you just come on in?" I asked him.

No sooner were the words out of my mouth than LoPresti, who had stolen up beside me by coming through the connecting door, snatched the towel and before I knew it had pushed me out into the hall and slammed my door and locked it. Demaret meanwhile had dashed down to the door to the connecting room and slammed the door behind him. There stood Penna stark naked in the hall, right in front of where the elevators were busily going up and down.

Fortunately none of the elevators stopped at our floor immediately and I looked frantically around for a place to conceal myself. The only thing I could see was a very small broom closet where the maid on the floor kept a mop and a bucket.

I opened the door and kicked the bucket out into the hallway but, despite my small stature, the closet still wasn't large enough to completely conceal me.

So there I stood with a mop in my hand and at that moment the elevator door a short way down the hall opened and three ladies emerged and started in my direction.

Squeezing myself as far into the tiny closet as I could and pulling the door toward me as much as possible, I held the mop in the vicinity of my missing belt buckle.

One of the ladies looked at me in wide-eyed amazement and the only thing I could think of to say was:

"Good afternoon, madame."

All this did was add to my confusion because it attracted the studied attention of all three women, and they went on their way down the hall tittering loudly.

When they were out of view, I took the mop handle and began to beat a tattoo on the door to my room. Inside I could hear those three idiots howling gleefully.

"Open up the door or I'm gonna bust it down," I yelled.

At that juncture the elevator doors opened again and I made a hurried retreat to my too-shallow foxhole in the mop closet. This time it was a man, by himself, and as he started by me I said to him: "Hey, Mac, do me a favor and call the house detective."

Toney Penna, Mickey Rooney and Fred Astaire, Lakeside Golf Course, Hollywood, California

He stared at me open-mouthed as if I was a raving lunatic.

"I'm not nuts," I told him. "Those idiots I'm rooming with have locked me out of the room and I can't get back in."

"Okay." The guy grinned. "I'll send the cavalry right away."

After a few minutes that seemed like an hour the elevator doors opened again and a man with all the unmistakable earmarks of a house detective came trundling down the hall.

Looking me over from bare toes to mop to uncombed hair and back again, he demanded, "What's going on here?"

For one second I thought of belting him right in the kisser with the mop.

"Just get the door to that room open right over there," I said, pointing to my locked door. "And if you don't open it pretty quick, Buster, I'm going to break it down."

Just as he opened the door, the elevator doors opened again, and a crowd of women emerged. I almost went through him getting into my room.

The three others were still howling in the other room, and they had been smart enough to lock the connecting door, or all three of them might have had their obituaries written that afternoon.

Demaret long was a man who had a reputation of wearing extremely colorful clothing. Personally, I never considered him a fashion plate but I must admit that he was certainly colorful. I liked clothes and always carried a number of outfits when we were on the tour but Jimmy toted enough outfits to stock a small men's store. Thus, I still get a great chuckle out of the period when he was in the Navy during World War II and was stationed at the Bainbridge, Maryland, Naval Station.

On one occasion I went to New York for a week and decided that I would call Jimmy at Bainbridge and ask him if he couldn't get a weekend pass and come up and stay with me a few days.

"Sure, I think I can pull it off," Demaret said on the phone.

He said that he would arrive at the McAlpin Hotel, where I was staying, on Friday evening. He was as good as his word and, that evening, there was a knock on the door and when I opened it there stood Jimmy.

As I pointed out, when Jimmy was on the tour, there hardly was enough room in the automobile for all his clothing.

Now, this night at the McAlpin, there stood Jimmy in the doorway in his swabbie blues holding in his hand one of those small men's shaving kits.

"Where are your bags?" I asked him.

He dangled the little bag in front of me by its handle.

"Here I am, pal." He smiled.

"Well, for crying out loud," I said, "you are going to stay for the weekend, aren't you?"

"Of course," he replied, "certainly I'm going to stay for the weekend."

"Well, where are your clothes?"

Once again he held the little bag up in front of me. "This is my gear."

"You mean to tell me that you're going to spend the weekend with me and that's all you have?" I asked him.

Jimmy's smile seemed to spread from ear to ear.

"Hell, yes, I can go around the world with this little bag," he told me. "Don't you know, man, I'm in the Navy now?"

He sure enough was. Because after we came in from a round of the night clubs at about four in the morning, Jimmy Demaret, a clothes fancier par excellence, went into the bathroom and washed out his T-shirt so that he could wear it the next day.

As I have said, I have always been quite the man for hot, flashy automobiles. I also long have been a Buick man, primarily due to my friendship with Rollie Withers, general sales manager for Buick.

I'll never forget the time I drove my new Buick Century up in front of the Sacramento Hotel where I was to stay during the play of the Sacramento Open. I left the automobile right in front of the main entrance and went in to the desk to register.

"Son," I told the bellboy, "will you please go out front to that new Buick and bring in my bags."

The boy left and came back moments later with a puzzled look on his face.

"If there was a Buick out there in front it sure isn't there now," he said.

"Well, just come with me and I'll show you," I told him.

But the boy was right. For when I went out through the main entrance my car was gone. In a mild panic I rushed through the parking area looking for it in case someone had merely moved it out of the way. But nowhere was my new car to be seen. This was not to be taken lightly, not only because the automobile was brand-new, but also because it contained all my clothes, clubs, balls and other supplies.

After rushing back into the hotel I called the police department and reported that my car had been stolen.

Within a few moments a police car drove up in front of the hotel and the chief of police came over to me.

"Mr. Penna," the chief asked me, "just where did you leave your car?"

"Right here where you're standing," I told him.

"Let me see your driver's license and your registration," he demanded.

"Well," I stumbled, "they are in the glove compartment of the car."

"Are you quite sure you had a car when you arrived?" he asked me. "Don't you know you are supposed to keep your license and your registration on your person?"

Within a few moments he had me feeling as if I had never even owned an automobile. But when, at about that time, I saw Tommy LoPresti stroll nonchalantly out through the front door of the hotel I knew that this was just another cooked-up gag to make Penna blow his stack.

"Okay," I said to LoPresti. "Enough is enough, where is the car?"

LoPresti and the chief both broke up. I felt like helping them.

As it developed, LoPresti was walking up to the hotel when he saw me leave the car to go check in. He had taken my car and driven it three blocks away to the police station and cooked up the whole gag with the chief of police.

My younger brother, Charlie, as I have said, is the head professional at the Beverly Country Club in Chicago. Quite a few times, whenever I was in Chicago, we would put on an exhibition at his club. Of course, Charlie and I never teed it up without a little wager going on the side, but the money had to be put up, because if I lost I never paid him and if he lost he never would pay me.

During one of these exhibitions, Craig Wood and I played Charlie and Bill Kerr, who at that time was president of the Beverly Country Club. We played a fifty-dollar Nassau, and Craig and I had our brains knocked out. Craig developed a miserable case of the putting yips. He at that time was playing as fine a game of golf as you would ever want to see from tee to green, but it is indicative of our play that day that he hit seventeen greens in regulation and yet scored an 84.

So Charlie with a wicked grin picked up my three hundred dollars. Now, this didn't strike me as the way things ought to turn out, considering that we had never before ever paid each other off. And what rubbed me the wrong way, on top of this, was that Charlie was gloating over the fact that he had actually nicked me for three hundred dollars.

Anyhow the following week I was playing well in the World Championship at Tam O' Shanter in Chicago and was making a good run at the lead. There were no ropes and Charlie was in my gallery, walking down the fairway beside me.

I had a good shot at winning the tournament, yet, strange as it may seem, all I could think about was how I could get my three hundred bucks back from Charlie.

This was one of the biggest tournaments of the year and Charlie was quite excited at how well I was playing.

But that three hundred dollars kept cropping up in my mind and, noting how excited Charlie was, I figured he wouldn't be thinking too quickly. He was all wrapped up in about how I was going to play the next shot, whether I would go for the pin or for the fat part of the green or what I would do.

I engaged him in conversation designed to increase his excitement and then finally I said to him abruptly:

"Say, I tried to cash a check this morning for three hundred dollars and wasn't able to do it. I owe a fellow over there some money and he wants it right away.

Would you loan me a little cash until I get into the clubhouse?"

Charlie dug right down and peeled off three one-hundred-dollar bills.

I snatched them out of his hand, grinned right in his face, and Charlie knew that he had been "had."

"Thanks, old buddy," I told him.

Charlie just shook his head and walked a few feet away from me.

In connection with those tremendous tournaments at Tam O' Shanter, I have always felt that the golfing world should build a monument in memory of George May. He had the foresight to realize the benefits and assets that the game of golf could give to his business, it is true, and he realized many benefits from it. Yet, I have to think that it was May who was responsible for putting the game of golf into the big money brackets.

In taking belated stock of my competitive career, I long since have realized that my explosive temper kept me from being a consistent winner on the tour. A steady, easy-going personality is even more in demand in these times when the purses have become so fantastically large.

Which brings me to the time I signed George Bayer as a member of the MacGregor staff.

George at that time was a car salesman in Pasadena, California. I had heard a great deal about him from Bob Hope. It was Hope's opinion that Bayer, a two-hundred-forty pounder who stands six feet, five inches, could drive a golf ball farther than any man who ever lived. The first time I met him, through Hope, was at the Celebrities' Golf Tournament at Washington, D. C., in 1954. Hope had sponsored Bayer to play in the Celebrities' and asked me to look him over.

We took him out on the first tee after he was through playing his first round and I was in a "show me" mood. It didn't take me very long to see that Hope was right. Bayer in recent years has attempted to harness his power but he certainly is the longest hitter that ever appeared in the game of golf.

I invited George to have dinner with Hope and Del Webb, former owner of the New York Yankees baseball team who was playing in the pro-am part of the tournament. Del and I had played together in just about every pro-am preceding the Phoenix Open.

I already had determined that I was going to sign Bayer, if possible, because I figured that his tremendous hitting power would attract a tremendous following.

During the course of dinner I proceeded to give big George a tremendous needling. What I wanted to find out was whether he could take it. Hope kept kicking me under the table until I felt as if I was bruised from instep to kneecap. Throughout my inquisition, Bayer remained calm, smiling and unaffected.

After dinner Hope took me aside and asked: "What's the matter with you, are you nuts?"

I grinned at him. "What do you mean?"

"Is that the way you sign up people?" Hope asked me.

"Are you trying to destroy his morale or run him out of town?"

"Look, Bob," I told Hope, "this isn't just a matter of merely signing him. Maybe you don't know it but when you break in on the pro tour the way this game is played today you have to be able to take that long, sharp needle that everybody shooting for the big jackpots has out for the newcomer."

Hope looked very puzzled.

"I didn't know Bayer from Adam's off ox," I added. "All I knew was that he was a car salesman out of Pasadena who could wallop the ball. What do you think my company would say if I went back and told them that I'm signing up a car salesman without knowing anything about his personality."

One thing I will have to admit, it's a good thing for Toney Penna that big George was such an easy-going, pleasant fellow. Otherwise, he might have reached right across that table and flung little Toney into the next county. But, as it developed, I knew we were getting a fine gentleman as well as a good player who had the potential to become a great player.

OF MEN, NO MICE

There are many occasions on which I am asked how the game differs now compared with the past eras.

I would say there are two major differences.

The first is spelled m-o-n-e-y. When I was on the tour we were playing practically for peanuts. In the current era there hardly is a week in which there is not a tournament somewhere or other and at the current writing there is more than two million five hundred thousand dollars at stake in the course of the year, with the figure expected to increase from year to year.

Then, too, outside interests have become a major source of income through television appearances, exhibitions and endorsements.

The second factor is simply that the professional golfer of today is a lot smarter than we were. We were primarily graduates of the caddy ranks. I do not say this disparagingly. It was simply the economics of our day. We had to acquire our polish by association with people of other walks of life, learning from the bankers and brokers and other cultured members of the country clubs at which we served.

Today your professional golfer in the main is a college graduate. Consider, if you will, just a few of our staff members.

Jack Nicklaus is a product of Ohio State University.

George Bayer was a baseball pitcher, basketball player and a football player at the University of Washington. Big George signed a contract with the Washington Redskins of the National Football League before a knee injury ended his football days.

Mike Souchak was an All-Southern end at Duke University; Jacky Cupit went to the University of Houston; Wes Ellis won the Southwest Conference Golf Championship while at the University of Texas and completed his pre-med course before deciding on a golf career. Lionel Hebert majored in music at Louisiana State University.

During the height of my tournament career we had a great deal of time on our hands simply because tournament golf was, you might say, in its infancy. Endorsements were, on the whole, minuscule. Thus, during the course of a tournament, we had a great deal more time to loaf around the locker room or the grille room and fraternize with each other or with the club members.

We were invited into the homes of the socially prominent for cocktails and dinner on a great many occasions and yet, compared to today, we spent a great deal of time fraternizing among ourselves.

In my era, as I have pointed out before, there were far fewer tournaments and the players were not accompanied as frequently by their wives and families. Today they are on the road so constantly that they feel obligated to take their wives and children along with them. There was, not too far back, a "trailer era." It seemed as if almost every player on the tour was traveling by trailer with his family.

This was found to be too exhausting for both player and family and currently, though many travel by automobile, the majority prefer to fly and stay in motels or hotels. A great number of them also are invited into fine homes because golf has made them tremendous celebrities.

Therefore you do not find the golfer of today sitting around the locker room until midnight. These are fairway businessmen. They are not averse to socializing in the locker room but they simply do not have the time for it. There are lawyers who handle their affairs and with whom they must meet and then it is off to the wife and kiddies.

As an indication of how times have changed, Arnold Palmer and Jack Nicklaus both earned more than one hundred thousand dollars each last year in tournament winnings alone. Jack's leading money total for 1964 was one hundred thirteen thousand two hundred eighty-four dollars in official money alone. By "official" money, the P.G.A. means merely the money won in officially sanctioned tournaments. This does not include money which he earned in pro-ams, the British Open, in winning the individual international trophy in the Canada Cup matches or in exhibitions. It would be a fair estimate, I think, that with his golf clubs alone, Nicklaus probably earned as much as one hundred fifty thousand dollars. Bear in mind, too, that he earns a fantastic amount of money through his endorsements of various products.

By comparison, consider the fact that I signed Ben Hogan to a MacGregor contract in 1937 for a mere two hundred and fifty dollars.

It must be kept in mind, of course, that Hogan at that time had shown no trace of golfing genius and, as a matter of fact, was getting pretty well discouraged with the whole business. But Henry Picard, one of the top performers at that time, advised me that Hogan was not with any company and had all the talent to become a world-beater.

"I certainly would sign him up if I were you," Picard told me.

This was during the Hollywood Open in Hollywood, Florida, and I went to Ben and offered him the two hundred and fifty dollars to become a staff member for MacGregor. Indicative of the times, Hogan accepted it without the slightest hesitation. As I say, money has been probably the major change in golf.

Ben Hogan was affiliated with us for more than thirteen years before he decided to go into business for himself. Along with Hogan, we signed some other truly great champions for what today would be laughable sums. They included such as Byron Nelson, Jug McSpaden and Jackie Burke, Jr. Jackie came along somewhat later than most of the others and yet, for our five hundred dollars' investment, he proved himself a great credit to MacGregor, winning the Masters and the P.G.A. Championship both, in 1956, and a number of other tournaments before and afterwards.

Jackie and Demaret now are partners in the Champions Golf Club in Houston, Texas.

Speaking of Hogan, I have to feel that one of the things which remains unchanged in tournament golf is the keen competition which you will find in any tournament. There is an old line saying, "Write anything you want about me but be sure to spell the name right." I never felt this way.

In 1947, I shot a bitter 40 to lose the Los Angeles Open to Ben Hogan. There was nobody close to us and, it being one of those days when I simply didn't have it, I just blew the tournament.

I was completely outraged when one of the writers covering the tournament wrote a story that Toney Penna, executive vice president of the MacGregor Golf Company, had scored a 40 purposely to lose the tournament to one of MacGregor's tournament stars. I'd have taken a wedge to this guy's toupee if he had been around when I read the story, because it was completely ridiculous. However, we decided not to make a federal case out of it and just ignored the whole thing.

Yet it rankled deep inside me and I was in a slow burn for weeks. As luck would have it, that summer Hogan was the defending champion in the P.G.A. Championship at Plum Hollow Country Club in Detroit.

In those days, MacGregor annually held a party which it called the Tourney Club party for the press, dignitaries, officials and players as well as their wives. The party ordinarily was held the night before the first round of play. In those days the P.G.A. Championship was held at match play, meaning that two players would meet each other on a hole-by-hole basis and the field, thus, was halved with every round.

Naturally, we would have the opening round pairings brought up and posted on a large board so that everyone at the party could be informed as to which players were meeting each other and the times at which they teed off.

On this night, curious as to whom I was to play in the first round, I strolled up to the board to look it over. Hogan, as the defending champion, was teeing off first. And I was quite surprised to see that Hogan was playing none other than Toney Penna.

As I stood there, a large man who needed a shave and who was chewing on a cigar butt came up beside me and, looking up at the board, began to call of odds on all of the matches.

Ben Hogan, 1942 (Wide World)

"Hogan against Penna, eight to one," he said.

As he started on down the line, naming odds on each pairing, I tapped him on the shoulder and asked him, "What did you say the top match was?"

"You mean Hogan against Penna?"

I nodded.

He obviously did not know me and he said, "Oh, about eight to one."

"Great," I told him, "I'll take five hundred dollars' worth of that."

He looked at me quizzically. "Say, that's an awful lot of money. I don't know whether I can go for that kind of action or not. Would you take a little five to one?"

"Okay, I'll take five hundred dollars' worth at five to one," I said to him. "It doesn't make much difference to me, I just want a bet on that match."

He told me to wait right there for a few minutes and he would come back with the money.

"Get your money up in the meantime and the game is on," he told me.

I waited and a few minutes later back he came and, having met these types of characters before, I told him that we would put the money in escrow with the manager of the hotel. He agreed and, as he had said, "the game was on."

It didn't take long for the word to get around and in no time at all I was cornered by Craig Wood and Ernie Saybarac, both of whom then were affiliated with Mac-Gregor, as well as Tom "T-Bone" Robbins, who had come out from New York to attend our party and see the tournament. They all wanted a piece of the action. Maybe they didn't quite like my chances of beating Hogan but they sure did like the odds. So I gave each of them a piece of the wager.

We were to tee off at 8 A.M. the next day so I had arranged to leave for the course at seven o'clock. By the time my car arrived, there were Craig, Ernie and Tom all waiting to ride out with me. They weren't going to miss seeing their horse go into action.

We teed off with heavy dew still on the grass and the gallery consisted of Craig, Ernie, Tom and the two caddies.

My chances looked anything but bright when Hogan started off with four birdies in a row. The first thing I knew I was two down.

I won't go into the match in too much detail, but while Hogan needed a four on the eighteenth hole —which was never played—for a 67 he belonged to little Toney, three and one. Because a four on that last hole would have given me a 64.

The thing which did it was not merely the fact that anytime I have the Penna money on the line, I'm hot to trot. I also kept remembering that story about how I had supposedly thrown the Los Angeles Open to Hogan earlier that year.

In my personal rankings of golf's all-time greats, which you will see in a later chapter in this book, I make Hogan no worse than third in the whole history of the game. He was a great champion, one of the finest players that ever lived, bar none. The real old-timers talk about the classic swing of Harry Vardon, but no one can knock Hogan's mechanics to me.

Yet one of the greatest requisites which made him such a great champion, I learned in that particular match at Plum Hollow that day on which I was fortunate enough to beat him in the first round of the P.G.A. Championship.

As we teed off on the seventeenth hole, a five par, Ben was two down to me with two holes to play. What happened on that hole is conclusive evidence to me of the bulldog type of game he played and the uncompromising relentlessness which never permitted him to concede defeat until the last putt was holed.

I was on the green six feet behind the hole in three, putting for a birdie four. He was twenty feet behind the hole in four and putting for a par five.

Ben still was far outside of me, and yet he concentrated on that long putt as if it was the difference between victory and defeat. If he managed to sink it, he would have a par five, and I would merely need two putts from six feet to defeat him two and one. He putted within inches of the hole and had a tap-in for a bogey six.

There I lay, a scant six feet from the cup, and needed to get down in only two putts for victory.

Any ordinary competitor would have knocked my ball away and said, "Congratulations, let's go have a drink."

Not Hogan.

He stood back, nailing me with those razor-blade blue eyes, and waited for me to hole out.

It was a very satisfactory moment—and compensation for that insulting story in Los Angeles—as I stroked the ball gently and saw it plop into the hole for a birdie which beat Hogan three and one.

As I said, someone else might have kicked the ball out of the way. Not Ben. I don't know what ever went through his mind during the course of a tournament, win or lose, and I don't think anyone else ever did. Maybe he thought that lightning might strike me, or something else. I just wouldn't have any idea. But you could always say about Ben Hogan that as long as he had a possible chance he considered that he was "alive" and still could win whatever match he was playing.

Another incident which to me accentuates his implacable will to win and his feeling that he alone was the man to beat concerns an exhibition in which Demaret and I were playing a charity match against Hogan and Byron Nelson.

The match had been arranged by Jim Rhodes, governor of Ohio as this is written and a great friend of golf, and was played at Scioto Country Club in Columbus, Ohio.

One of the members at the club approached us on the first tee and said:

"I'd like to see this as an all-out match, even though it is an exhibition. If you fellows will hole out all of your putts, not giving each other those short ones, I will put up a two-hundred-dollar prize for the low man."

While this was a match for charity, actually nothing was at stake. So, on the way down the first fairway, I suggested to the three others that we just split up the two hundred dollars, giving each man fifty dollars, although naturally we all would shoot the best score possible and hole all of our putts.

Hogan looked at me with a wry grin.

"Nothing doing," he said. "No split. Let's just play for the two hundred dollars. The man who has the low score gets the two hundred bucks and that's it."

Demaret and Nelson said they were perfectly willing to go along with my plan but Hogan shook his head adamantly and repeated, "No split."

Possibly I am oversensitive. But Ben made me feel as if I was almost trying to pull off a shady deal. The old Penna temper began to rise up and to say that I was "hot" is to put it mildly.

In the old days something like this would have made me blow sky-high as far as my scoring was concerned. But now, instead, I had the same cold, bitter feeling which I had when I defeated Ben at Plum Hollow in the first round of the P.G.A. Championship.

Anyhow, when we holed out the final putt on the eighteenth green, the two hundred dollars went to the fellow who had scored a nice, neat 69.

A fellow by the name of Toney Penna.

THE CELEBRI-TEES

I wouldn't take a million dollars for my life in the wonderful game of golf. It staggers me when I consider the doors that this sport opened up for a boy who emigrated from Italy, started as a caddy and then went into club manufacturing because he had to learn a trade.

This game has permitted me to associate with royalty, sportsmen from all walks of life, presidents, vice presidents and other governmental dignitaries and figures in the entertainment world such as Bing Crosby, Bob Hope, Perry Como, Fred Astaire, Dean Martin, Frank Sinatra, Phil Harris, Lou Clayton and, yes, even that overgrown moose Toots Shor.

Being associated with people such as these had a vast influence on my life. According to current standards I was not very well educated and yet I was able to learn by associating with these people, observing their manners and mannerisms and listening to their advice. I owe a great deal to those who were kind enough to help me, especially when they saw me making a mistake. I have always considered those people as real friends who criticized my mistakes in a kindly manner.

Fred Astaire was one of the first celebrities I ever met and he had a great deal of influence on me. We met and played at the Bel Air Country Club and soon became fast friends. Fred did a great deal to help me acquire a certain savoir-faire. He was quite a student of the game of golf and played very well. As a matter of fact, the dancing man had a very rhythmic swing and, in his younger days, scored well, shooting generally in the high seventies. Fred and I played a great deal together, quite often with actor Randolph Scott, another fine player.

Bing Crosby and Bob Hope have been noted for years as golfing rivals. I met Crosby at Lakeside Golf Club, where he was the club champion, and I like to feel I had a great deal to do with him starting the Bing Crosby Pro-Amateur Invitational at Del Mar Golf Club.

Crosby, of course, had the money to spare and the tax situation was quite different in those days. So it was that I proposed to him that he put on his own tournament and he seized on the idea vigorously.

As a result, I played with Bing in each of the first

Phil Harris and Bing Crosby, Las Vegas, Nevada, 1959
(Wide World)

couple of tournaments until the P.G.A. suggested that it would be better for the tournament if Bing would play with the defending champion in the ensuing years. This he did, until he finally stopped competing in the tournament proper.

As to his own game, Bing played well enough to qualify on one occasion for the National Amateur Golf Championship. If he could have hit the ball twenty to thirty yards farther, he could have been one of the country's top amateurs. Even so, he was a tough competitor to beat, because even with his lack of distance he was a deadly match player.

Bing was in his glory when he was out there beating your brains out for a five-dollar or a ten-dollar Nassau. He would rather hustle me for a five-dollar Nassau, and see my dago temper flare, than anybody I've ever known in my life. He really loved to get the old man's neck red.

In the entertainment world, Bing is known as "the Groaner." Strangely enough, it was coined on the golf course. When his game went sour, Bing would groan and complain as if the world was coming to an end. It was as a result of this that his cronies began calling him "the Groaner."

Bing loved golf and golfers and every now and then, particularly in former years, when he had time enough to get away from his commitments he would show up at some golf tournament or other.

One year at the Texas Open, in San Antonio, we had cooked up a birthday party for Jimmy Demaret, and took over a small night club just on the outskirts of the city. Bing arrived in the city unannounced. He called me and I told him about the party.

"Suppose I show up and sing a couple of numbers in Jimmy's honor?" he asked me.

"Great."

A little later I told Jimmy, who sings pretty well himself, that he might have a little competition at the microphone that evening.

"I've invited a fellow who I think might even be able to outsing you, so you'd better polish up your tonsils a little bit," I told him.

Jimmy, of course, didn't have the slightest idea who it was but, during the course of the evening when dinner was getting around to the dessert stage, I went up on the stage and rattled the trap drums a bit. The curtain parted and there stood Crosby.

So it was that Bing sang a few numbers for Jimmy's birthday, songs which at that time probably were valued at about twenty thousand dollars a member. All this for free, just because of Bing's friendship and his love for the game of golf.

Bob Hope, I think, should be known as the Mister World of Golf. I don't know of any place in the world in which Bob hasn't struck a golf ball, whether it was desert or jungle. Everywhere he goes, there's a golf club with Hope.

It is well known how far and exhaustingly he travels for charity and to entertain servicemen. But the first thing he does when he gets back from a tiring trip is to take off for the golf course. I met Hope during one of the early Crosby pro-ams and, naturally being onstage most of the time, he's a real panic in any foursome.

Hope loves the game with a passion and his greatest fault always has been with his golf grip. If he ever had taken the time to improve his grip he'd have been a really fine player. He knows the game through and through, as much, I would say, as almost any pro I know of. If you start talking about the swing and the game with Hope, you had better have the proper answers, because he knows what he's talking about at all times.

I first met Perry Como in the late thirties when I went to St. Louis to play an exhibition against a couple of archers, in one of those goofy affairs in which I hit the ball with golf clubs and they shot arrows until they reached the cup.

Perry was at that time working with Ted Weems's band and came out to see the match. I don't even recall how the match came out but we hit it right off the bat and we've been friends ever since, not because I was Italian-born and he was of Italian extraction, but due to his love of the game.

Perry is one of the greatest students of the game I have ever known and has a beautiful, smooth golf swing. He plays exceptionally well, getting it down into the low seventies as a general rule. I'm quite certain that if Perry had the time, he would turn professional if he could.

Perry Como, Toney Penna, West Palm Beach, Florida, 1958
(Wide World)

For sheer fun and laughs you have to go a long way to match Phil Harris. Demaret nicknamed him "Harley-Davidson," because Phil fiddles more with his hands while he's trying to get his grip and before he hits a golf shot than anybody I know.

"He looks like a man twisting the throttles on the handlebars of a motorcycle," said Demaret. "This fellow looks as if he is riding a Harley-Davidson."

Thus did Harris become "Harley-Davidson."

Harris is a dedicated banana ball player; meaning that everything's a fade. On top of this he sticks with nothing but woods when he is playing toward the green. I do not think that Harris has ever played toward the green with anything higher than a four-iron. From a four-iron he jumps to a five-wood which we at MacGregor made specially for him. He calls it his "little moneymaker" because he plays it so well and we have "moneymaker" stamped right on the head in gold letters. I think he probably would eat with this club if he could.

One of the most generous and thoughtful of all those I have been privileged to meet or to play golf with was Lou Clayton of the Clayton and Durante team a few years back. I spent a great deal of time with him as his guest when the winter tour was in action on the west coast. There was a period when I could not walk into a restaurant and have dinner, with friends or alone, and sign a check.

"I can't be this well known," I said to myself.

I wasn't. Lou Clayton had left orders in most of the places we frequented:

"Anytime Toney Penna walks into this place, pick up the check and send me the bill."

It wasn't until years later that I learned he had issued those orders.

Lou was a comedian, on or off the golf course, and didn't give a hang about a twenty-dollar Nassau unless everybody was having fun. I have to thank Lou Clayton for teaching me not only how to travel top drawer but also how to thoroughly enjoy myself.

I am extremely humble when I think of my origin and how golf gave me the opportunity to meet such a man as former vice president Richard Nixon.

When he first took office he made a visit to Del Ray Beach, where I lived for a number of years, and it was there that he first seriously began to play golf. I have been associated with him since that time, as far as golf goes, and I consider his friendship something that I shall cherish as long as I live. He has become a keen student of the game and quite a fair player as well. I have found him to be a kind and considerate man and never will forget how, because his shoes were a bit dirty after playing golf, he took them off and left them on the front porch before walking into the house in his stockinged feet.

At the time my daughter was working on a thesis concerning Communism. When he heard what she was doing he sat down and patiently helped her with various ideas and enlightened her on various facets of the subject.

She won a prize for it, too.

Dean Martin's knees almost touch the ground when he swings through the golf ball. I had been told, before I played with him the first time, that he was a "tip seeker" who always wanted to know what any pro with whom he was playing thought of his swing, grip or stance.

I didn't say a word to him, by design, but I could see that he was very anxious after about six holes for me to say something concerning his golf game.

When I didn't he got tired of waiting and said:

"What's the matter, you don't talk when you play golf?"

I merely shrugged.

"Well, okay, what's wrong with my golf game?" he asked me.

I looked at him with a sidewise glance and, talking out of the side of my mouth, said:

"You're the only player I ever saw that swung at a golf ball and genuflected at the same time."

With that, everybody broke up, including Martin, who has a great sense of humor.

One of the greatest personalities I ever met in my life is Frank Sinatra. This guy, without the slightest doubt, I'd rather have on my side anytime than walking against me, because if he is your friend he is really your friend. Frank didn't take up the game until recent years and I believe that if he would make up his mind to take it seriously he would play a decent game.

But Sinatra is as casual about golf as he is in front of a microphone. He goes out on the golf course and if things don't go too well he'll toss the stick to the caddy and say:

"Let's go, gents, I'm off to the nearest bar."

Golf opened all types of doors for me, not just those to the stars but also those to industrial giants and men in practically every field.

For example, through golf I became very well acquainted with Chick Allyn, former president of the National Cash Register Company. We became quite friendly when I was working in Dayton, Ohio, where our MacGregor Golf Company first began manufacturing golf clubs.

He became so interested in golf that he became president of the P.G.A. Advisory Board and ran one of the finest P.G.A. championships in which I've ever had the pleasure of playing.

Another close friend through golf, and one with whom I'm associated in a public relations manner, is Johnny McHugh, of the McHugh Construction Company. Because of him, whenever I go into the big town of Chicago, the red carpet is always rolled out, which is really something to an ex-caddy who once spoke fractured English.

How can I thank this game enough for meeting a man such as Johnny McGuire, vice president of the

Thor Tool Company which manufactures pneumatic tools?

Johnny undoubtedly is one of the greatest golf addicts in the world and one of the best customers golf ever had. If I held a job at a club in any part of the country and I had ten Johnny McGuires for members, that's all I would need, because Johnny has probably bought more golf clubs than any one person in the history of the game.

Another golfing fanatic is Larry McQueen, executive vice president of the General Tire and Rubber Company. He is probably one of the worst players I've ever seen in my life, although he shoots between 80 and 85. He uses an eight-wood to go thirty yards over a bunker and never attempts to use a sand iron. But his greatest recreation on the golf course is to play with me and criticize my "lousy golf swing."

But I can always look and laugh back at him and say: "Come on, hit the ball up there with that lousy eight-wood of yours."

Then there are men such as Donald Hardenbrook, vice president of the Union Paper Bag Company. Donald loves golfing technique and would rather look good playing golf than anybody I know of. He'd rather fan it than hit a really good golf shot if, in the process, he looked good doing it. As a matter of fact, he was influential in causing me to design our MT golf clubs.

Hardenbrook loved thick-bladed irons because, he insisted, they convey to him a feeling of power, and his

Bo Wininger, Frank Sinatra, Toney Penna (Bill Mark)

insistence started me tinkering with what eventually became our MT line.

The guys who can grin whether they hit it toward the hole or hit it out of bounds are the greatest fun to play with and one of the greatest in this department is Al Heimann. Al is the man who makes me look good on the golf course. He is in the tailoring business, owns a lot of clothing companies in the Cincinnati area and he has seen to it over the years that I was well-dressed on the golf course, even if I wasn't playing well.

Golf, and all sports for that matter, owe a towering debt to Toots Shor, one of the never-ending boosters of sport of every description. This big moose had to have a special set of clubs made for him because, I think, he was unwilling to take off his money belt.

He made me measure him for a set of clubs right in the middle of his restaurant one year, and then, whacking me so hard with one of his platter-sized hands that I almost hit the deck, trumpeted:

"You better get the specifications right, little man, or don't dare come back to town."

Actually he knew next to nothing about a golf club or even the game of golf. I don't know of anyone who plays much worse, but to hear him talk you'd think he was Ben Hogan and Bobby Jones combined.

Another of those who helped me a great deal in my club-designing career was Larry Lloyd, who was associated with a now-defunct golf club manufacturing company when you and I were young, Maggie. Larry was a key figure in the creation of the new Deepdale Golf Club, which Dick Wilson built on Long Island. It is one of the finest of many splendid courses in the New York area.

Women's play has mushroomed so fantastically over the past few years that MacGregor, in addition to its men's advisory staff, also has a women's staff of girls who play on the Ladies' P.G.A. tour. They include such stars as Marlene Hagge, Ruth Jessen, Barbara Romack, Sandra Spuzich, Louise Suggs and Sherry Wheeler.

One of our early staff members was the late and great Mildred (Babe) Didrikson Zaharias. A woman with almost unbelievable athletic talent, the Babe had been an Olympic track star and she turned professional after a number of amateur golf victories. She still needed work on various parts of her game to fit the professional pattern and she was turned over to me for instruction. I worked with her and played a number of exhibitions with her for a period of about three months and then, feeling that she needed still more work and not having the time to devote to her exclusively, I turned her over to Tommy Armour.

Eventually she became the greatest woman player of her time and did a great deal to popularize women's golf before her untimely death.

The sportswriters always have been nice to me and I would like to pay a tribute to their inestimable contribution to the game of golf. There are, of course, a great many of them but those with whom I worked most closely were such as Red Smith, Larry Robinson and Joe Williams of New York; Guido Cribari of the Westchester papers; Herb Graffis and Charley Bartlett of Chicago; Jimmy Burns of Miami; Bob Balfe of West Palm Beach, Florida; Shirley Povich and Francis Stann of Washington; Hal Wood of the Honolulu *Advertiser;* Whitney Martin of the Associated Press; Tom Fitzgerald and Joe Looney of Boston; John Ross of *Golf Magazine,* and Dick Taylor and the late Bob Harlow of *Golf World.*

Without golf I would never have been honored to know such fine people from all walks of life. To me it is a million-dollar world and I wouldn't take ten million dollars for it.

"DOCTORING" THE PROS

You undoubtedly have been told, or have read countless times, that if you are having trouble with your golf game you should obtain instruction from a qualified golf professional. I'm not trying to beat a dead horse, but let's look at it this way.

For example, a doctor may prescribe for himself in case of a minor ailment, but when he gets extreme symptoms he goes to another doctor who can view his case dispassionately. Dentists get toothaches just as you and I. They can't fill their own cavities so they go to another dentist. There is an old saying in the legal profession that the lawyer who acts as his own attorney has a fool for counsel.

A golf professional is no different. When his game goes sour he needs outside help.

In this connection, I long have been a golf pro's "doctor."

I have been observing golf pros and their individual idiosyncrasies for a number of years and many, many times while I was playing on the tour various professionals, especially boys who were on our staff and realized that I knew their game through and through, would come to me for help.

It always is important to us that our staff members play well and make a good showing in tournament competition. We created a staff for our MacGregor Golf Company to serve as a show window of golf for the public as well as to act in the capacity of good-will ambassadors as far as the industry is concerned.

Yet I have never turned down a request from the staff member of another company for help. My reasoning is that any player, whether he was on our staff or that of another company, who helped in any way to create good will for the game itself was in the long run creating golf customers of which MacGregor would get its share.

This same reasoning applied to our own staff. No matter how much we had to pay them, if we thought they helped to promote not only the game but also an increase in the followers of golf, they were well worth while, no matter what it cost us to have them affiliated with our company.

Our staff through the years has been one of the finest playing staffs the game has ever known, with such stars as Ben Hogan, Byron Nelson, Jimmy Demaret, Jug McSpaden and Dick Metz, right up to such present-day stars as Jack Nicklaus, Mike Souchak, George Bayer and Lionel Hebert, just to name a few. Nicklaus, I sincerely believe, probably will be unbeatable for the next decade and to my thinking is the finest player I have ever been fortunate enough to watch throughout my many years in golf. More of him later.

But to return to my theme, while these boys all are wonderful players, there isn't a single one of them who doesn't go to a fellow professional for help at one time or another.

Nicklaus recently disclosed that he had received a great deal of help from Ralph Hutchinson of Saucon Valley as well as from George Lowe, a putting wizard.

I am highly flattered that frequently I am approached by one or another of today's top players for assistance. In the case of a golf doctor, you must be able to go beyond the mere mechanics of the swing and be father confessor as well as psychologist and psychoanalyst.

Mike Souchak is a perfect example of what I am attempting to explain, and I'm quite certain he wouldn't mind my talking about him.

I have had Mike come to me just before he went to the practice tee to loosen up for a round in a tournament and complain that he was hooking or fading or driving poorly or not really getting into the ball.

I know Mike's game as well as that of anyone else in golf because I watched him grow from a pup and have been following his game with unwavering attention for almost fifteen years.

My first thought always in a case like this is not to confuse him with too many suggestions and, if possible, make him think, for the sake of his own confidence, that he actually has worked out his own solution.

After all, he is about to tee off with a great deal of money at stake and confusion can only lead to disaster. Thus when Mike comes to me and complains he is having a bit of difficulty I go out on the practice tee and watch him hit a few shots for possibly five to fifteen minutes, and I do not attempt to convey a single thought of any kind to him until I am certain that the first thing I hit him with is something which would positively produce in him a good feeling and get him in a good frame of mind before he tees off.

I reiterate, he is going out there to play for a great deal of money and I do not want to produce in him or contribute in any way to any more confusion.

After watching, and as I said, knowing his game thoroughly, I can spot the key fault which is causing all his golfing ailments. Let's say, as an example, without ever realizing it he has fallen into an open stance.

Then I will suggest:

"Mike, last year when you were playing so well during the Texas Open you were standing at the ball a little bit differently. I think you're a little more open and your hips are open too. I believe if you'll just close them up you'll get into your swing better."

Mike is a very strong player and he meets the ball real firm and hard.

Sam Snead, La Quinta, California, 1964 (Wide World)

He is not too much on finesse. This means that when he gets up there and hits the ball with a firm, strong swing, he has his game at its peak of production. Therefore his confusion dissolves and he again is capable of positive thinking.

As I say, when you go to a doctor, you do what he tells you to do.

Mike will think over such a suggestion and give it a try. He possibly hasn't realized what his trouble was stemming from because even a doctor at times needs someone else to look at him. All Mike realizes is that all of a sudden he is hitting the ball the way he knows he can hit it.

At this point I'll watch him a few more minutes to see that he has settled back into his groove and then I quietly slip away. He doesn't need me anymore and anything else I said would only confuse him at a point where he feels he already has been cured.

There is, without question, a broad mental side to golf.

Let's consider Mike again. There was a time in the spring of 1964 when he was on the verge of quitting tournament golf. He hadn't been able to win a tournament in almost three years and he was in a blue funk. He had discussed the situation with his lovely wife, Nancy.

"I'd just like to give it one more try," he told her dejectedly. "I know I can still be a winner."

Nancy went along with him all the way.

"Any way you want it is all right with me," she said loyally.

Mike still was troubled and confused when he arrived at the Masters that spring. He posted a couple of good rounds but then again had finished poorly.

I felt that the only trouble with Mike was in his head, that his confidence had deserted him and he still had a sound, winning swing. All he needed was for somebody to talk to him like a Dutch uncle.

So we sat down, he and Nancy and I, and we had a long straight-from-the-shoulder talk.

"Mike, I know what you want deep down in your heart," I told him. "You want to finish out what you started to do, and that's to be a true champion. You haven't won a tournament now in almost three years and it has gotten deep under your skin. Once you make up your mind that you are a real champion and that you can play winning golf you will lose this confusion which is destroying you."

We talked for a long time and I related many incidents about the time when he was winning and why at those times he was playing so well. We discussed fully why he had not won two United States Open Championships which he might have won. He lost to Billy Casper at Winged Foot in 1959 and to Arnold Palmer at Cherry Hills in 1960 when he could have captured both of them.

At Cherry Hills, Mike was leading in the third round when on the eighteenth hole a spectator snapped his picture just as Mike reached the top of his backswing and started down. It upset Mike's rhythm and he hit the ball out of bounds. Mike never recovered his composure.

"Nobody wins the Open," I told him. "The rest of the field loses it. But you must gear yourself mentally to forget the bad breaks and constantly remind yourself that you are a champion."

All that Mike had needed was to talk the uncertainty out of himself and regain his faith in his golfing ability. The feeling that Nancy and I believed implicitly in him did the trick.

He went right out and won the Houston Classic and the Memphis Open.

I had been hoping that Mike might accept a permanent job with MacGregor as my assistant and eventual successor. But I talked him right out of the job.

Jackie Burke is another who comes to mind when I speak of being a doctor's doctor, or a pro's pro. I have always admired Jackie's golf game ever since I met him when he was a youngster at River Oaks Country Club in Houston, where I long had been a friend of his father's.

Every time I think of Jackie I recall his first meeting with Bob Hope.

Jackie, when he became a professional at eighteen, had an extremely boyish appearance.

The first time he was introduced to Hope they shook hands and Hope asked him:

"What do you do, son?"

"I'm a golf professional," Jackie told him.

Hope looked at him with banjo-eyed surprise and blurted:

"A golf pro? Where, Boys' Town?"

But Jackie always has had as fine a golf swing as there is in the game.

His one weakness as far as I could determine was in his grip. Burke usually was in a state of confusion concerning his grip.

He had been around Jimmy Demaret so long that he thought he could play like him. However, I don't know of anyone who ever had a pair of hands like Demaret when he wraps them around a golf club. Jimmy's left hand always has been very weak and his right hand exceptionally strong, which made him play with a short, three-quarter swing. But he could manipulate the club like an artist through the hitting area.

Jackie simply was not able to play that way. His finest playing always was done with a two-knuckle grip and a strong left hand on his club where he could take a free, full turn and a good, flowing swing.

I hammered at him constantly and any time he would see me around he would become conscious of it and play with his full swing.

On those occasions when Jackie Burke came to me for advice we would walk out on the practice tee and in most cases he simply wasn't turning enough to get the full potential of his individual golf swing.

Each person must play his own game, to utilize the strong points of his personal physique and swing. It is an old adage that one man's dish is another man's poison but it certainly fits in golf.

Consider, if you will, the case of Gardner Dickinson, who is one of our MacGregor staff members.

Gardner had been working for Ben Hogan as well as playing golf with Hogan a great deal and he admired Ben so much that he copied his style and his every move, right down to the point of dressing the same way.

But changing his style almost ruined Gardner's game. He was playing poorly on the tour and, having a wife and three children, he either had to win or else go back to a club job to support them. I told him if he was going to stay on the tour he would have to make an awful lot of changes in his game.

I looked at some pictures of Gardner's former style and said:

"Why don't you just go back to your own natural way of playing?"

He was attempting to play with a very weak left hand, which meant that he was fading the ball à la Hogan. Gardner is small of stature and even though he is quite strong it wasn't a natural style of play for him as he attempted to ape Ben.

"Gardner," I advised him, "your natural way of playing according to the pictures taken when you were younger is to take a big, long swing with a strong left hand which permits you to cock your hands well underneath the shaft at the top of the backswing."

I could see that he was listening intently and analyzing thoroughly what I was saying.

I added: "You're not only going to hit the ball longer, but you're going to hit the ball straighter and you'll be stronger throughout your whole game."

He agreed to give it a try and the proof is in the pudding because the next year he had one of the most successful money-winning tours of his entire career.

George Bayer probably had one of the greatest potentials as a golfer of anybody I've ever seen in my life, not only because of his long hitting and his tremendous strength, but also because of a fine attitude.

Yet, I am sorry to say, George never did acquire his full potential simply because he never took time enough to acquire a fine grip on the golf club.

George has a large, remarkable pair of hands and yet he plays with what I personally consider to be one of the worst grips I've ever seen in golf.

His hands have never been united on the grip. They always come apart and it is only through his strength and natural golf swing that he has done as well as he has. If George Bayer had ever taken time enough to acquire a real fine grip he would have been not only a sensationally long driver, but also a much straighter driver. I'm certain that he would have gone on to many more victories than he has attained.

Even now it isn't too late. Should George ever take

time out actually to work on his grip and improve it, I think he could go on to be a major winner. But he has never taken the time and no matter how much he tries to work on improving his grip between tournaments, the grip that he has used practically all of his life has become such sound second nature to him that it's practically impossible for him to acquire a fine grip. He's been told not only by me but also by many other friends of his.

At this stage it would take two months or maybe more for him to develop the feel and confidence a new grip would require and George doesn't think he can afford to change over and miss a chance at the giant jackpots in the interim.

All I can say is, I never knew a doctor who won every case, either.

PRO-TYPE TIPS

t this point I would like to give you what I consider pro-type tips concerning your own game.

First let me say that there are a million instruction books on the market aimed at the absolute beginner who never has played the game of golf. The basic preliminaries, how to stand, how to hold the club, and how to swing probably can be learned from these excellent books which are on the whole authored by tournament stars whose names will attract book store attention, and I, too, will give it the once-over lightly in the next chapter.

I hold, however, that the average person cannot learn to play good golf in this manner. As an example, Jack Nicklaus can tell you how he plays the game but it might not fit your own individual case. First of all, as far as I am concerned, there is only one Jack Nicklaus.

What I am getting at is that I contend with unwavering insistence that there is absolutely no substitute for learning the basic fundamentals from a club professional, just as I have asserted in the beginning that you cannot be perfectly fitted for clubs without the aid of an expert who knows exactly what he is doing.

Naturally those who are just starting to play golf are of particular importance to us at MacGregor because, feeling that we design and manufacture the finest clubs in the world, we cherish the beginner as a potential customer. Yet I must reiterate, do yourself a lasting favor if you stand in this category and see a professional for your basic instruction.

Thus here I am aiming my remarks at those who already play, who may have a glaring weakness which baffles them or who do not feel that they are getting the most out of their particular potential on the golf course.

In this chapter you will find a chart which I have devised and which I feel gives you a general cause and cure analysis that may be of inestimable aid if you are suffering from some golfing ailment or other. As I must keep repeating, a golfer should visit a professional for a check-up on his game just as a man sees his doctor for a physical check-up. I have told this to many older players. And they have found that a few major points generally need correction before they become incurable.

The response to this advice of mine has been surprising. Senior golfers said that a few little errors had crept into their games and were eliminated after a few minutes with a golf professional, who diagnosed the illness and provided the cure. The professionals who had helped these seniors later discussed with me how a few corrections could improve the game of golfers of all ages.

The nimble, strong, and muscularly responsive young golfer can, and usually does, respond very well on the lesson tee. But the seniors need different treatment. About the best method is to suggest to them a couple of corrective routines every few rounds so that the player can concentrate on them individually.

Most professionals find, however, that the major problem is to get the veteran player to stop in for a periodical check-up. When I was a home club professional, I believed that if the grip of my members could be regularly checked, and minor adjustments made, their scoring would improve.

However, as players will not go to their professionals as often as they should, the only alternative was to take the check-up to the player. That effort is made by me with the accompanying chart.

In it you will find that the common complaints of golfers are listed at the top of the various pages. Factors which may account for these errors are in the column on the left. The cures that work, in most cases, are briefly listed in the right column on each page.

I am certain from my experiences as a teacher that the recommended treatments usually will be successful.

If not, the chances are that the patient *thinks* he is doing what is prescribed, but actually he is not following through on what is suggested.

It is my belief that the best way to take full advantage of this chart is to go over it with your own club professional.

Just as an example of how it works, let's consider the grip, which I have always considered to be the most important part of the golf game.

Look at the first chart page which is titled "Slicing."

If you are a chronic slicer, according to the chart you will see that all you must do is move your left hand more to the right on the grip of the club and the right hand more under the shaft.

Conversely, if you are hooking, you merely move the right hand to the top of the grip, with one knuckle of the left hand and two of the right visible to you.

All right, so you are topping the ball. This may be due to many things, as you will see in the chart, including position, body weight distribution, foot action, the position of your head, or what you are doing with your arms or with your timing.

All of these factors come into play no matter what your problem may be. But I always prefer to start with the grip. Thus, if you are topping the ball, check your grip to make certain that you are not letting loose with the left hand.

If you are hitting behind the ball, again let us check the grip first. This, in effect, is caused by the same fault

TONEY PENNA'S
CAUSE AND CURE CHART

 # SLICING

GRIP	Move left hand more to right on the grip and the right hand more under the shaft.
POSITION	Bring right foot back from line of flight and into a closed stance.
BODY	Keep weight evenly distributed instead of falling back. Throughout the swing the body must work with the hands: not ahead or behind.
FOOT ACTION	Firm, towards balls of feet. Feet must be as live as hands. Left foot action starts backswing. Right heel must get off ground in downswing. Right knee bends toward left leg in downswing.
HEAD POSITION	Steady but not rigid. Fix attention on back of ball where contact should be made, instead of vaguely "keeping eye on the ball."
ARMS	Left arm should be well extended but not stiff, so arc of swing will not change. Right elbow must be kept pointing down.
TIMING	Don't start hitting from top of backswing. Delay hand action instead of being too eager.

 # HOOKING

GRIP	Move right hand more on top of grip, with one knuckle of left hand and two of right visible to you.
POSITION	Slightly open or square stance. You cannot hook if your weight is on the right foot.
BODY	Move the left side out of the way on backswing and downswing.
FOOT ACTION	Have weight favoring right foot but not so much that leg and body action will be stiff.
HEAD POSITION	Keep head steadily behind the ball. Turning the head a little to the right at address may help.
ARMS	Keep left arm extended and let both arms go toward the flag after the ball is hit.
TIMING	Moving ball forward or back with relation to stance may help.

 # TOPPING

GRIP	Correct your grip so you won't let loose with the left hand.
POSITION	Ball may be too close to the right foot. Knees probably are too stiff instead of being unlocked and even bent a little during most of the swing.
BODY	Perhaps the body has moved ahead of the arms and hands.
FOOT ACTION	Too much weight on left foot at address and never got off of leaning on the left so a properly balanced swing could be made.
HEAD POSITION	Looking at the top of the ball instead of the back axis of the ball which is the correct target.
ARMS	Left arm may have been bent and length of the arc are changed during the swing.
TIMING	Usually too fast on backswing and jerkiness is developed.

 # HITTING BEHIND THE BALL

GRIP	Same grip fault as in topping. Left hand is too loose.
POSITION	Ball too close to left foot in address.
BODY	You may have swayed back and forth instead of shifting weight and turning the body.
FOOT ACTION	Feet have stayed flat instead of moving.
HEAD POSITION	Head moves back away from the ball.
ARMS	Chopping from the top instead of swinging at the ball.
TIMING	Backswing too fast and too fast on delivery instead of waiting. Timing usually is O.K. when it is not rushed.

 # SHANKING

GRIP	Any grip fault; too strong or too weak with either hand. Then the player tries to adjust during his swing and with disastrous results.
POSITION	You can shank from any stance or with ball in any position with relation to your feet.
BODY	Leaning on toes instead of being firmly but not rigidly set on the balls of the feet.
FOOT ACTION	Flat-footed or using only one foot. Both feet should be moved in co-ordination with the hands.
HEAD POSITION	Scared and nervous and the head shifts and bobs instead of being kept steady.
ARMS	Arms are back of alignment with the face of the club.
TIMING	Fast backswing without a good timing pause at top of the swing.

 # SHORT SHOTS FROM BUNKERS

GRIP	Take normal grip then turn hands so back of left hand is horizontal.
POSITION	For normal lie in sand play ball off left heel. Very open stance.
BODY	Hold the body still.
FOOT ACTION	Feet planted solidly. Play the shot flat-footed, it's a hand and arm shot.
HEAD POSITION	Steadily behind the ball. Keep attention directed on spot in sand back of ball where club is to hit.
ARMS	Firm, extended left arm and very little wrist action. Follow through.
TIMING	Play the shot leisurely, in waltz time.

 **LACK OF DISTANCE**

GRIP	Hands close together and working as unit. Strong grip but not tense.
POSITION	Closed stance. Stand up to the ball rather than stooping or squatting.
BODY	Full body turn to make a long arc of the swing. Set left side of body soldily before arms move from top of swing.
FOOT ACTION	Lot of foot action to get full body turn. Must be smoothly geared to arm and hand action.
HEAD POSITION	Must be kept well behind the ball. If you move head ahead of the ball, you can't hit the ball hard.
ARMS	Left arm fully extended and full cocking of wrists at the top.
TIMING	Hands must be kept ahead of the clubhead so wrist action produces greatest clubhead speed at contact. Rushing the shot results in jerky action and loss of power.

in your grip as if you are topping the ball. In other words, your left hand grip is too loose.

Let's say that you are shanking the ball. This can be due to any fault in your grip: too strong or too weak with either hand. Then you must try to adjust during the swing and you are obtaining disastrous results.

A great many people feel that they are not getting anywhere near the distance which they should. Once again this may have started with your grip. In this case you must try to get your hands closer together and working as a unit. A strong grip is necessary but remember, never become tense.

As I have said in using this chart, always start, no matter what your difficulty, with checking every facet of your grip. From there in using the chart you go on to your position at the ball, your body weight distribution, your foot action, your head position, how you are using your arms and finally to your timing.

By cross checking all the way through this chart I feel quite certain that you will hit sooner or later upon the key factor which is causing your problems.

I do not say this because I formulated this chart, but I do feel that if you will study it you will find it of tremendous value.

I would like to go on from here and give you my opinion on golf as it may be played more effectively as well as some pertinent "tips" which I am thoroughly convinced will be of prime assistance to the average player.

Let's first of all face the fact that there is such a tremendous amount of words written, in magazines and books, that the average player seeking information or corrective aid has to wind up in a complete state of shock and confusion. What you are reading, as personalities and methods change is, as I said, how this star or that plays and before you know it you are bogged down in the mental mire of too many suggested points. It is, in a manner of speaking, like using parts from a dozen different automobiles and trying to make the product look like a Rolls-Royce. Of course it is an impossibility. It is equally impossible with your golf game.

What I am driving at is that you don't have to be a Jack Nicklaus or a Mike Souchak, or perform technically as they do, to play an enjoyable game of golf which fits your own particular abilities and brings out the highest potentials of your own possibly limited skills.

I say "limited" because, unless golf is your business or unless you have the time to play every day, while you may without knowing it have all the potential of a championship contender, your lack of time to practice legislates against your ever reaching your true capabilities. So it is that, due to lack of time, you are what is known as an average player.

Golf, therefore, is an escape from the humdrum activities of your daily or business life.

You have read, like the pros, before you tee off you

should spend and hour hitting through your whole set of clubs on the practice tee. Then, it is said, spend fifteen to twenty minutes on the putting green. Sure, the pros do it and it is with them an absolute necessity.

But golf is their business. To you this game is an escape, a release from the chains of business. Time to you is precious in other fields. You want to arrive at the club, tee it up and start whacking your way around the course. If it is a day on which you feel exceptionally well and the morning has been productive, you are adjusted mentally and the physical part of you is ready, able, and willing to comply.

Ideally, if you have the time, a check-up once or twice a month under the knowing eye of your club professional will pay marvelous dividends. And, in these lessons make certain that he is picking out your one greatest weakness and not confusing you with a dozen "don'ts." Correcting that one key error usually will efface the others that you are making in the process.

But for those unable to do this, I would have to say you should attain comfort in your swing and develop your feel into the hitting area. This sums up the entire manner in which you can obtain the most from your own individual game.

As far as the swing is concerned, there is no such thing as a standard. All of us are built differently and habits are hard to change. In the case of the swing consider tribulations of such tournament players as Ed Furgol and Jim Ferrier. Furgol suffered an injury in boyhood which left him with a rigid and withered left arm. Certainly he could not become a stylist. Yet, as one of the finest shot makers I have ever seen, he won among other titles the most prized one of them all, the U. S. Open Championship. Ferrier because of a knee injury dips incredibly during his swing but, like Furgol, he worked on his own individual style until he had perfected it. He did this so well that he captured many events including the P. G. A. Championship.

The answer is that you, as they did, must compensate for weaknesses. Let's say that you are a good driver but cannot hit good long irons with any effectiveness. There can be no doubt, in such a case, that you unconsciously are changing your stance or your swing or making changes in some manner. How can you help yourself? Well, analyze what you are doing when you drive well and determine if and how you are changing when you go to your long irons.

In essence what I am advocating is that you start with the strongest part of your game and tailor the rest of your game to this strength.

You face the same situation when it comes to gripping the club. Too many times to count, I have been asked by this person or that whether they should use the Vardon overlapping grip, the interlocking grip, or what. My answer never varies.

Use the grip which feels the most comfortable to you because you must grip for "feel."

Consider, as an example, how many and how various

are the grips which are used by the leading professionals on the golf tour.

Bob Rosburg uses what is referred to as a "baseball" grip. With this grip he has all ten fingers on the shaft and the hands are slightly separated. It is not actually a baseball grip but the left hand is well over the top of the shaft and the right hand is more underneath than is orthodox. However, Bob manages to play exceedingly well and a proof of that is that he, too, is a former champion of the Professional Golfers Association.

Then there is Doug Ford. He plays with what I refer to as a hook grip, with a very strong left hand. He manages to offset this by using a flat swing. Little Jerry Barber has a very strong left hand grip and what I consider to be a weak right hand grip. However, he offsets this with a solid grip as he comes through the hitting area. Art Wall, who won the Masters Championship uses a ten finger grip which differs from Rosburg's and yet he is a beautiful player.

Before going into a few pointed "tips" I'd like to say that if there is one most valuable hint I could give to any player it would be to check his stance very frequently. You should, on the whole, play with a perfectly even stance as far as your line of flight is concerned. You can do this very easily by placing a club on the ground so that it touches the tip of each toe as you take your stance. Then you can walk away and sight down the club and see whether you are standing on the line of flight which you intend to take. I suggest that even good players should use this check point quite frequently. As I said earlier, even the finest of tournament players such as Mike Souchak face off in the wrong direction without realizing it.

Stand squarely toward the ball, with your hips, shoulders, and feet even and your weight equally distributed so that if someone shoved a chair under you you would sit down very evenly.

As to my "tips" I think you will find that if you apply the five following principles you cannot help but take shots off your game:

1. Play the percentage shots.
2. Analyze the hole and play to its weakness.
3. Visualize your shot and play to your own capabilities.
4. Chip with as straight-faced a club as is possible.
5. Putt in your own way and the one which is most comfortable.

Let's consider these principles one by one.

You might almost say that points one and two are interlocking. Because when I refer to the percentage shot this has a great deal to do with analyzing the hole and playing to its weakness.

However, let's, as an example, say that you come to a short hole where the others in your group are all whipping out irons for their shots. If you do not think you can reach the green with an iron, don't, by any means, be ashamed to take a wood.

If your ego needs bolstering, merely remember little

Arnold Palmer and caddy, Augusta, Georgia, 1964
(Wide World)

Paul Runyan. He won the P. G. A. Championship twice. In 1934 he outlasted Craig Wood by beating him on the 38th hole at the country club of Buffalo and in 1938 he won the championship again by beating Sam Snead mercilessly, 8 and 7, at Shawnee-on-Delaware. Runyan was a very short hitter but, in both cases, he bested both Wood and Snead with his four wood. Both of his rivals could outdrive him but Runyan was death with that little four wood.

Along this same line, band leader Fred Waring plays with an entire set of woods while Phil Harris, as I explained earlier, never uses more than a four iron and from there picks his teeth and everybody's wallet with that five wood which he calls his "Little Money Maker."

Making the proper club selection has a great deal to do with playing to the weakness of a hole instead of to its strength. What you are trying to do here is to select the club which will give you the least penalty if you miss the shot. One such instance would be the 13th hole at the Masters at Augusta National Golf Club. Here the hole has a water hazard in the front reaching to the right side. It also is heavily trapped to the left side and back of the green. Unless they can cut the corner with surgical precision, even the long hitting pros are content to lay up short of all that trouble for a safe third shot to the green. In other words, don't gamble when the odds are stacked heavily against you.

Another example at the Augusta National would be the 11th hole. If you go to the left you are in the water.

You can go as much as 100 yards to the right and not be in any extreme difficulty. Therefore, in such a situation, you obviously should play to the right side and eliminate flirting with the hazard of going into the water.

It's much like fighting a boxer who has a good left hook and a weak right hand. What any professional boxer would do in such an instance would be to circle away from his opponent's Sunday punch.

Golf is much the same.

One of the most important tips I could ever give any player is that which I have labeled Number 3, Visualizing your shot and playing it to your capabilities.

The first thing you must realize is that you are not a professional. You have attended tournaments and seen the pros fly a shot right to the pin and make it stick. Certainly you would love to hit this type of shot. But, if you are an average and occasional player, then the thing to do is to hit the shot you know you can hit.

How many times have you double or triple bogeyed a hole and then, after putting out on the green, look disconsolately back at what should be an easy hole to at least bogey and figure out that you could have played it better if you had struck every shot with a putter?

What you failed to do and what sent your score soaring was to blueprint the hole so that you were playing shots which you knew you were capable of playing.

Let's again consider a long par five hole where you have gotten off one of your best drives and tied in a fairly good second shot. You know that if you hit one of your "career" shots you just might make it to the green. In most cases you will not be able to resist the temptation so you blast away, regardless of those yawning traps guarding the green, and probably dump it right on the beach.

How much better, in retrospect, if you had played the shot neatly short of the green, flipped it up and given yourself to maybe get home in one putt for your par.

Instead, you are buried in the bunker and only Heaven knows what will happen next. The odds are that you will come off with a seven or maybe worse.

In this connection I have seen average players who play the same course day in and day out and never are able to improve on their scores because they are continually making the same mistakes as far as club selection, judgment of distance and refusal to play the shot they know they can hit.

Even your finest professionals never constantly go for the pin.

Ben Hogan was one of the finest "readers" of a golf course I have ever seen. He could play one practice round and he would have all of the landmarks on the course etched into his brain and would fit his game to the potential of the course. Nobody could change his opinion and this was one of the reasons for his greatness.

Two examples might be the 13th and 15th holes at

the Masters. A greater percentage of the field always plays these holes short, rather than slugging away desperately in an attempt to reach the green. The reason is that the hazards and the penalty they will exact far outweigh the little bit of profit which will be gained by a desperation shot to the green which might come off, and probably wouldn't.

Watch the professionals carefully, not just thrilling to the perfect shots, and you will discover how many of them deliberately are playing the present shot to set up the one ahead. And, the greater percentage of the time, they are playing the safe shot which is aimed at the weakness of the course and will leave them without trouble.

The reason that the hacker shoots in the high 90's or has trouble breaking 100 is because he ignores the hazards and tries to plow his way through them. How much better if he plays short of those traps or short of that lake and then leaves himself a little pitch for a possible par and no more than a bogey if it comes off that way instead of killing a 6, 7, 8, or even more.

Another example would be the 16th hole at Cypress Point. I have stood there in amazement and watched hackers try to reach this green which seems to be located in the middle of the ocean. The 16th, as you probably know, is a par 3 hole and it can be played very safely to the left with an iron and leaves only a chip to the green.

However, the brave ones can aim straight at the pin

and knock it over an inlet of the ocean. Miss the shot, as most average players do, and you still are standing on the tee but now you are shooting three. Playing it the safe way, with an iron to the left and a chip to the green, almost anyone might get down in three but certainly would hole out in four. Much, much better than standing on the tee shooting three.

Now let's move along to point 4, in which I suggest that you chip with as straight a faced club as possible.

As a general rule I would say never chip and run with a club which has more loft than a seven iron. And, on top of this, drop down as much as possible all the way to the putter.

The reason for this is that when you get up to the eight and the nine irons for your chipping, you are losing a great deal of your accuracy as well as distance control. Distance of course must come with "feel." The best hint I could give you, barring enough play to obtain accurate feel, would be to strike the ball as hard as you would for a putt of the same distance.

I must hold however that the putter should be used as much as possible.

The putter is known in the Southwest, where the courses are baked hard and dry, as the "Texas Wedge." This is because it is used in the scoring area of 50 yards from the green.

I recall one instance in which Jug McSpaden shot a 59 at Breckenridge Park in San Antonio in which he used the putter from 50 yards out on practically every occasion because the greens and the aprons were so hard.

Certainly this is a prime testimonial to what can be accomplished with the putter.

I would suggest that the average player use the putter even out of bunkers if it is possible, meaning if there is no overhanging lip to impede the path of the ball. What you want to do is to be sure to get it out of the hazard.

I have seen a great many wonderful players leave the ball in these bunkers.

Take, for instance, Arnold Palmer's misfortune in the 1961 Masters at Augusta National.

Palmer needed a par four to win the championship but his approach shot landed in a bunker at the green.

Palmer took a wedge and exploded the ball and even this great champion, under the conditions, knocked it clean over the green.

He wound up with a double bogey six and lost by one slender shot to Gary Player.

If Arnold could have rolled it out of there with his putter, he certainly would have done so. Because his percentage shot was to get it on the green from that bunker and give himself an opportunity to hole out in one for victory or at least to get it down in two strokes for a tie which would have forced a play-off but still left him alive.

Concerning my fifth point, I have always been a stylist. However, when it comes to putting I yield to the man who can get it in the hole in the fewest strokes even if he does it standing on his head.

Putting is all "feel" and the rest of it is in your head.

Therefore, I say use the stance and the grip which are most comfortable and most productive for you and don't let anyone in the world talk you out of them.

Talk of putting methods always reminds me of the time when Bobby Cruickshank and Tommy Armour went to Australia for the Australian Open Golf Championship.

There was a tremendously large putting clock, or practice green, in Sydney, and Cruickshank went there one day alone.

Bobby was one of the finest putters the game ever produced, having a beautiful, sensitive pendulum stroke.

While he was on this putting green in Sydney, Bobby was rather amused to see an elderly lady of about seventy years of age putting the ball back and forth.

He fell into conversation with her and she told him, rather proudly, that she considered herself one of the best putters in the world.

Bobby watched her and had difficulty restraining his laughter. Because this elderly lady would merely put the putter down behind the ball, look at the hole, and then putt without even looking at the ball.

As a gag, Cruickshank challenged her to a little match. She accepted willingly.

Not only that, she beat him soundly.

As I contended, putting a great deal of the time is in your head.

Bobby was so amazed at the way this elderly lady could knock the ball into the hole that he adopted her putting style.

When he returned to the United States, one of his first appearances was in the Los Angeles Open at Rancho Country Club and, using the putting style he had copied from the elderly lady in Sydney, he fired a brilliant 67 in the first round. Still using her putting method of merely placing the blade behind the ball, looking at the hole and then striking the ball without even looking at it, he shot a 69 in the second round.

Then, in the third round, he was paired with Armour,

Cruickshank's new putting style by this time was the center of conversation among the tournament professionals.

Armour was patently unimpressed and he had a sharp needle all ready for Cruickshank when they met the next day.

"I understand you are taking lessons from little old ladies." He laughed. "Well, Bobby, you're going to have to show me."

Trying to hide his pique, Cruickshank went into his new putting system on the very first green. He placed the blade behind the ball, looked squarely at the hole and then struck down without looking at the ball.

It is sad to relate that Armour's needle had shattered Bobby's confidence.

The putter blade stubbed into the turf and the ball did not move an inch.

Cruickshank went forlornly back to his old way of putting.

It is to be doubted that the elderly lady's putting style would have held up on the professional tour, even though Cruickshank had fired two fine rounds by using it.

However, who is to say what it might have done for him if he had retained his confidence. Thus I repeat that the important thing is to be comfortable and use a putting style which you prefer and forget the jibes of anyone who may not concur with how you are striking the ball on the green. The pay-off undoubtedly will be in your favor.

If there would be one final point which I would make to the average golfer, it is to avoid tension as much as possible. Remember that you are out on the golf course to have a good time and even if you are blowing a $5 Nassau just be happy that you can be there.

Look up at God's blue sky, take a deep breath, and knock the hell out of it.

FOR THE BEGINNER

I have always held firmly that the absolute beginner in the game of golf would avoid many dangerous pitfalls and bad habits by starting out from scratch with lessons from a bonafide golf professional.

However, I realize that lack of time and/or money frequently makes this impossible for many people. Therefore, I feel I would be remiss if I did not give some thought and explanation to those who are just contemplating a start in the game.

First of all it is necessary for the novice to know that under the rules of golf you are permitted to carry only fourteen clubs in your bag.

This means that the standard set includes four wood clubs: the driver, the brassie or number two wood for your longer fairway shots when you have a good lie, the spoon or number three wood, and the number four wood.

There are also nine irons and a putter. The irons are classified as the long irons, meaning the number two and number three irons; the medium irons, the four, five, and six irons; and the short irons, the seven, eight, and nine irons. To this you will add a wedge, a heavy soled club used for playing out of sand or out of deep rough, and a putter.

This selection of clubs is varied greatly by any number of players. For instance, some players prefer to carry two wedges, one designed for playing from the rough and for approach shots and the other with a heavier sole, to handle their shots from bunkers. Still others prefer a special chipping iron or some may even carry two putters.

Therefore, something must be left out to stay within the fourteen club limit.

A great number of players leave out the brassie. Others prefer to dispose of the two iron. These personal combinations are so varied that it is impossible to go into them.

However, I feel that the average player who does not have a great deal of time for practice and plays only on occasion would do well to eliminate first of all the driver and the brassie as well as the two and three irons. The reason is that these are particularly difficult clubs to master.

Replacing them, I would suggest that the average player obtain a driver with a minimum loft of 11 degrees or more. A one and one half wood, for example, just may keep you from dribbling those tee shots off the tee because it gives you a better chance to get the ball up into the air. You also will find that a five wood will pay you tremendous dividends.

The driver is a particularly difficult club to use and you will see a great many players using a brassie off the tee. This is because the driver frustrates them completely. Yet, in substituting the brassie for the driver, they find that they are lofting the ball too much off the tee.

The brassie also is a very difficult club to use off the fairway unless you have a particularly lush lie.

Also, it will only give you a slight distance advantage over the three wood, which in turn is much easier for the average player to handle.

Now when I speak of the one and one half wood, I am not referring to a brassie. It still is a deep-faced driver but it has more added loft and gives you much more chance as I explained of getting the ball up into the air from the tee.

As to the five wood, this is a relatively new club and has been accepted widely by the average player because he can get the ball up with it so easily. Those long irons, the two and three irons, require a tremendous amount of practice to play them with any success. Even some of your professionals lack the timing which these longer shafted irons require and the margin of error is so great that the average player would do well to stay away from them.

Speaking generally of clubs, you can, like many professionals, carry two wedges. However, I believe that for the average person the double duty wedge designed for both play from sand and from the rough, as well as for your approach shots, is a highly satisfactory implement.

The wedge can be the duffer's best friend. Your average player most frequently misses the green by anywhere from ten to fifty yards with his approach shots. With a fair amount of experimentation and observation of how the ball reacts when it is struck with the wedge, he will find it one of the most satisfactory clubs in his bag. Get it up there to where you have a chance to one putt and you will save a great number of shots.

Remaining relaxed while learning how to play golf, and while playing, is one of the best suggestions anyone could make. You will always find that one of the major faults among the average golfers is that they are too tense and tied up muscularly while they are addressing the ball and this causes a great many players to hit the ball with the heel of the club.

Until you have grooved your swing, you will find, I think, that when swinging at the ball you are extending your arms more than when you are at address, meaning before you begin your swing. If you discover that this is happening to you, merely address the ball slightly off the tee of the club. Then, during your swing, your arms naturally will extend themselves and the ball will be contacted squarely on the face of the clubhead.

I think that there are three major checkpoints for the average player, keeping a straight left arm, keeping the right elbow in close to the side, and not lifting the left heel too far off the ground during the backswing.

Your left arm is the controlling factor in any good golf swing and the major fault of the average golfer is permitting the left arm to collapse either at the top of the backswing or as the downswing is started.

Many average golfers, and I would say this includes the majority of those who play the game, are cursed with a slice. This is a shot which starts out straight and then curves off to the right, ruining accuracy and causing in the process a great loss of distance. A slice is due to a great extent to the collapse of the left arm.

You must keep that left arm comfortably extended, firm but not rigid, throughout your swing. This permits you to maintain a wide arc, building up power, and grooving your swing. However, if you allow the left arm to collapse as you start your downswing, this will allow the right hand, the right arm, and the right side to take over the swing. This forces the club to move outside the correct line of your swing and pulls the clubhead across the intended line of flight from the outside to the inside, in contacting the ball. This imparts to the ball a sidewise, clockwise revolution which carries it off to the right in a looping flight which is known as a slice.

Another major factor which causes a slice is when you open the last two fingers of the left hand at the top of the backswing. Then, as you start your downswing, the hand tightens automatically and makes the clubhead loop, throwing it out of line and forcing it to come down across the ball for a slice. You might refer, at this point, to my "cause and cure" chart in the preceding chapter.

Another prime fault among the average players is raising the right elbow away from the body during the backswing. Here again you are causing the right side to take over and you are robbing yourself of a great deal of your hitting power.

I mentioned the fact that too many players raise the left heel too far off the ground at the top of their backswing.

This, of course, pulls your head away from its position over the ball. You will hear it said many times to "keep your eye on the ball." This is not necessarily so, considering the fact that there are many blind golfers who play the game exceptionally well despite their handicap. What they are trying to do when they tell you to "keep your eye on the ball" is to maintain the head in one position at the ball so that during your swing, both your backswing and your downswing, your body will pivot around your head. As long as it is kept in a fixed position your swing will remain in its groove. Naturally there is some slight movement but the head should be kept as stationary as possible at all times.

One method of checking this is to take your stance with the sun at your back and carefully observe whether the shadow of your head on the ground is moving when you swing.

The next time you have an opportunity to see a professional play, observe that he seldom raises his left heel more than one or at the most two inches off the ground. Actually, from the six iron down through the wedge almost all of them play these shots without the left heel leaving the ground at all.

THE GRIP

Most professionals will advocate one grip or another, the interlocking grip which means that your left forefinger is interlocked with the little finger of your right hand; the overlapping grip in which the little finger of your right hand overlaps the forefinger of your left hand or, more and more of late, the ten finger grip in which the hands are close together so that they can work as one unit and all ten fingers are on the shaft.

I contend that you should use the grip which feels the most comfortable to you.

However, I do contend also that no matter what grip you use your hands must be positioned properly. In placing your left hand on the grip of the club be certain that the club is held in the palm and fingers of the left hand and not just in the fingers. With the club resting diagonally across the palm, the V formed by the left thumb and forefinger should point directly to the right shoulder. Too often there is a tendency to open the left hand, by which it is meant that the hand is turned too far to the left so that the V points to the left shoulder. Making that left hand V point to the right shoulder may feel somewhat uncomfortable in the beginning but you will discover that it will keep the left hand working throughout your swing.

And, again, in connection with that left hand grip, remember that at the top of the backswing you must not relax that grip by the little finger because, as sure as you do, you will tighten it automatically as you start your downswing. This will cause you to regrip the club, and the net result could be almost anything: a slice, a hook or a topped shot. It all depends on how you close your hand back on the club.

As opposed to the left hand grip, the right hand is a complete finger grip. The V formed by the thumb and forefinger of the right hand should be parallel to the V formed by the left hand and should be pointing therefore to the right shoulder also. This coordinates the hands and keeps them working as a unit.

A bad grip has hurt more players than almost anything else I can think of in the game of golf.

I think you would find it vastly beneficial, as well as a great deal of fun, if you would go to a driving range or to your club's practice tee and experiment with positioning your hands in various ways. You soon will discover that there is only one proper position and that is the one which I have described.

Bobby Jones, New York City, 1953 (Wide World)

THE WOODS

The greatest danger the average player faces in trying to hit his woods is that he feels he must "kill" the ball. Actually, you will be surprised at how much farther and straighter you will hit the ball if you will concentrate on swinging smoothly and easily and letting the club do the work.

This is due to the fact that in using the woods, particularly the driver and brassie, they requrie exceptional timing because of your longer shaft and the necessarily wider arc which you are getting.

The major fault among most average players is that they are in too much of a hurry to wallop the ball and as result do not take enough time on their backswing. The general tendency is to rush the clubhead back and swing down at the ball as rapidly as possible. You cannot do this with your woods and hit them well.

If you rush the clubhead back and then lunge savagely down at the ball you are completely ruining not only your timing but also your balance. So, take them back slowly and feel that you are making a perceptible pause at the top of your backswing.

I am reminded of a story about Bobby Jones when he was playing in the U.S. Amateur Championship and was having trouble with his drives. Jones asked his home club professional, Stewart Maiden, to watch him on the practice tee. Maiden observed silently and then commented tersely:

"Why don't you hit it with your backswing?"

In other words, even the immortal Jones, as magnificently as he played the game, was destroying his rhythm by rushing his backswing. It is obviously a fault easy to get into.

With your driving club, the stance should be square to the line of flight. As I have mentioned it is a good idea occasionally to place a club on the ground so that it touches the toe of both shoes when you take your stance. Then sight along the club and make certain it is pointing directly toward your target. If one foot is withdrawn, then you are not facing properly.

Again with your driving club the ball should be played in a line with your left heel.

You start your swing back with a simultaneous turning of the hips as the arms take the clubhead back straight and low. At this point, you must be extremely careful that you do not pick up the clubhead with an immediate cocking of the wrists. The arms should be almost belt high before this wrist cock takes place, preserving your balance and setting up a pattern for your downswing. The left arm in the meantime is kept firmly extended with no bend to the left elbow and the right elbow is kept in close to the body.

To maintain perfect control of the club also be certain that you do not drop the clubhead below a horizontal line at the top of your backswing. If you do you are overswinging and you undoubtedly will lose control as you start your downswing.

There is some controversy as to whether the hips or the left heel lead the downswing. I prefer to think that it is a simultaneous movement with the hips and the left heel returning to the ground starting your downswing. The wrists remain cocked until the hands have returned to that belt line hitting area. Then, as the arms progress those last few inches which brings them into line with the ball, the wrists unleash their power and drive the clubhead into the ball.

One of the major faults of the average player is in failing to swing on through for a full finish which carries the hands high in completing the rhythmic arc of the swing. A great many poor players quit on their swing immediately after contacting the ball, ending their swing just a few feet past where the ball had been, instead of swinging on through and letting the full swing bring the head up naturally.

The brassie is played mechanically the same as the driving club.

You should find that the three wood is one of your best fairway weapons. First of all, being much lighter than the brassie, it is much less tiring for the average player to use. The mechanics of hitting the three wood are the same as with the longer woods but due to the shorter shaft the ball should be positioned slightly more toward the middle of the stance.

Actually, however, the four wood should be of even greater aid to the average player because he will not have the feeling that he must help the club "lift" the ball. The four wood is played in the same manner as the other woods but the ball should be positioned only a fraction ahead of the center line between the feet, again because of the slightly shorter shaft.

The five wood is a club which has come more and more into play. The reason here again is that it is much lighter and easier to swing with your weekend golfing muscles. Because of its still shorter shaft, the ball is played almost at the center line between the feet.

I have spoken to you about slicing and of course must also mention the other extreme which is hooking. In this case, the ball is curving from right to left after you have hit it and, while many professionals feel that a controlled hook gives them more distance, if you permit it to become a regular part of your game it can be just as devastating to your control as the slice.

In my "Cause and Cure" chart you will see many reasons why you may be hooking the ball unintentionally. One of the major factors is having too closed a stance, meaning that the right foot is pulled back too far from the intended line of flight.

On many occasions it also can be due to a faulty grip, in which the V's formed by the thumb and forefinger of your right hand point toward your right elbow instead of toward your right shoulder. In other words the grip of your right hand is too open.

DIFFICULT LIES

It is with the woods that you will be called upon to play many difficult lies, where you will be shooting up hill, down hill or side hill, in the latter case where the ball may be above your feet or below your feet. It is a good idea for the beginner to hit his shots from a level surface and not toy with these difficult lies until he is ready to play seriously.

In the case of the uphill lie, it is one where your left foot is on a higher plane than your right foot. Naturally this causes most of your weight to be thrown back on your right foot and therefore to provide better balance in your swing and equalize your weight distribution you merely bend your left knee slightly.

It also stands to reason that in hitting this uphill shot the ball will have more loft than you would normally obtain from the club you are using. Thus if you are hitting what would normally be a five iron shot, it is necessary to hit a four iron to compensate for the added loft. Also, due to the fact that your weight is thrown to the right side, there is a tendency to hook the ball. Therefore, it behooves you to aim slightly to the right of your objective and open your stance slightly.

The downhill lie quite naturally works just the opposite. In this case your weight would be primarily on your left leg and you would have a tendency to slice the ball.

In addressing the ball, the right knee should be bent slightly for better balance, the ball should be placed slightly behind the center line of your stance, and to combat that tendency to slice, it is well to aim a bit to the left of your objective.

Where in playing the uphill lie you use a club with

Gene Sarazen at the Delhi, India, Golf Club, 1964
(Wide World)

less loft, in playing the downhill lie you should use a club with more loft. This, as you can see, is due to the fact that you have trouble getting the ball up into the air because your position offsets part of the loft of the club you are using.

As I mentioned, your sidehill lie can be where the ball is higher than your feet or lower than your feet.

Common sense dictates what you do in such a situation. Let's say that the ball is higher than your feet. In this case you merely shorten your grip on the shaft. If the ball is lower than your feet, you must take a longer grip on your shaft.

In the case where the ball is below your feet, what you must do is bend your knees slightly and keep the weight on the heels to make certain that you do not fall into the shot. It is extremely vital that you stay down throughout your swing so that you do not top the ball. Another factor is that you should stand slightly closer to the ball than is normal in your own case.

In cases where the ball is higher than the feet, you merely reverse the procedure. You shorten your grip on the club, take your stance slightly farther away from the ball than usual, and keep your weight on the balls of your feet. In doing this you will not fall away from the shot as you swing through the ball.

LONG IRONS

The long irons, the two and three irons, are two of the most difficult clubs in the bag to hit. In essence, the swing is the same as is used in hitting the woods. There must be a full backswing and a complete pivot, although, because of the shorter shafts, you are standing closer to the ball than you are in using the woods.

If you have the time, master the long irons. They naturally have a vital part in a championship game. For example, the two iron will be much more productive than the four wood when you are hitting into the wind.

The reason is that the four wood will carry the ball higher into the air than the two iron. Thus the four wood shot can be more easily affected by the wind while the two iron shot provides less chance of interference from the wind.

In hitting either the two or the three iron, the stance is more narrow than in hitting the woods and the ball is played in closer to the body, as I have explained, because the shaft is not as long as those of the woods. One of the major faults in playing these long irons is that many people play the ball too far forward, while actually the ball should be positioned just ahead of the center line of the stance.

I think that the major factor legislating against good long iron play by your average player is the feeling that he must overpower the ball. If you will swing the club smoothly, taking a full pivot, keeping a firm grip and letting the clubhead do the work, your attempts to handle the long iron shots should not be as aggravating as they might be otherwise.

It is with the long irons that you will find yourself

making two major mistakes, either hitting behind the ball or topping it.

Hitting behind the ball can be caused by that feeling that you must overpower it when hitting the two or three irons. In attempting to hit it with all of your power, you probably will be falling into the ball, swaying your body, and thus moving your swing out of its groove. There is a possibility, too, that you will play the ball too far forward toward your left foot.

Topping the ball means that it either is being struck on the upswing or cut into on the downswing. There are any number of causes of topping, including trying to "lift" the ball, looking up, failing to pivot or, as I have said, playing the ball too far forward in your stance.

As a truer indication of how many factors can cause a fault in your game, let us consider topping the ball as explained in my "Cause and Cure" chart.

If you will look at the chart, you will see that it can be your grip, where you may be letting loose with your left hand. It can be your position, where the ball may be too close to the right foot or where the knees may be too stiff. It can be caused because your body has moved ahead of the arms and hands or it may be in your foot action, if you have too much weight on the left foot at address and thereby your swing is unbalanced. It could be your head position, where you are looking at the top of the ball instead of the back axis of the ball which is your correct target. It may be your arms, where your left arm collapsed and the length of your arc has changed during the swing. Again, it may be your timing, where your backswing is too fast and you are developing a jerky swing.

MEDIUM IRONS

The medium irons consist of the four, five, and six irons. Because the shafts become increasingly shorter, the ball naturally moves in closer to the feet and the swing becomes more upright.

One important factor here is that you must take your divot before you hit the ball. If you are striking the ground behind the ball you are wasting your power.

The key to your medium irons is keeping your left arm firm and straight and your right elbow in close to the side. In case of the four iron, the feet again are square to the line of flight and the ball should be played a trifle ahead of the center line between the feet.

The five iron is played identically with the ball positioned almost squarely between the feet. In the case of the six iron, the ball is played slightly back of that center line.

CHIP SHOTS

Chip shots can be played with any club from the four down through the nine iron and the wedge, depending on your personal choice.

What you must develop in hitting your chip shots is "feel," and because of this, and the average player's inabilty to practice with the entire set of clubs, I hold that it is better for the duffer to concentrate on two chipping clubs. Let's say, for example, the six iron and the wedge. You will develop more feel if you concentrate on two clubs and these two will do the job you find necessary. The seven iron can be used for running up the ball and the wedge can be used if you are behind a hazard.

In chipping, the feet should be fairly close together, with the weight equally distributed on both feet, and the hands should be positioned slightly ahead of the ball to assure that it will be struck a descending blow. Wrist action is kept to a minimum and the hands should be ahead of the clubhead all the way through the chip shot. It is a shot made with the arms and there is very little if any body movement.

How hard a chip shot should be struck for any particular distance must be determined through practice and observation. Generally, however, a run up chip shot should require about as much force as a putt of the same distance.

It is with the medium and the short irons that you may fall into the habit of what is known as shanking, meaning that the ball squirts off at a right angle.

This can be due to many facors. It may be due to a fault in your grip, where one hand overpowers the other and the player attempts to adjust during his swing. It may be because you have your weight too far on your toes, because you are playing flat-footed, because your head is shifting, because your arms are back of alignment with the face of the club or because of too fast a backswing, a swing which is too short or moving the head back and forward.

Any one of these can cause the clubhead to move out away from the body, driving the neck of the club into the ball for what is known as a shank.

SHORT IRONS

The short irons are the seven, eight, and nine irons, along with your wedges. Most of your average players find these the easiest clubs in the bag to hit and it demonstrates the necessity of being confident when you play golf. One factor which helps to produce this confidence undoubtedly is that the average player uses the short irons more than he does the other clubs, thereby gaining more ability and, in the process, more confidence. Your average player can hit the short irons better than any of the other clubs primarily because he can see more of the face, does not feel that he has to "lift" the ball, and therefore strikes with more authority.

With the short irons, the feet are closer together and the ball is played back behind the center line of the stance. The short irons are the ones on which it is important to have backspin so that the ball will hold the green. All that this requires is that you strike the ball first, with a downward blow, before taking your divot. Again let me remind you, as always, go on through with a full follow through. One vitally important factor in playing the short irons is that 80 per cent of the weight should be kept on the left side.

You may choose to use the eight or the nine iron for your pitch shots, meaning longer shots than the chip shots around the green and shots which usually must carry over a trap or some other type of hazard.

In the pitch shot, the ball is played off the right foot and the feet are closer together than in making the full short iron swing. There is very little body movement, if any, due to the fact that the pitch shot ordinarily is made with a half or three-quarter swing. The club is taken back with only the hands and arms and there is only a small amount of wrist cock. One of the major factors is a slow, smooth backswing. Actually, smoothness is the key to the whole business at hand.

As I said earlier, you may choose to play by carrying both a sand wedge and a pitching wedge but you may be able to develop more all around feel by using a double duty wedge designed for use from either bunker or fairway.

When pitching with the wedge, the ball is played off the right foot with a slightly open stance. This is to insure that you will contact the ball before the clubhead strikes the grass or the rough.

One of the best shots with the wedge, if you must make the ball stop quickly, is the cut shot.

In this shot the ball is positioned just inside the right foot with the stance very open so that the body is almost facing the hole. The face of the club is laid open and the ball is struck before taking the divot. The open stance makes certain that the club cuts across the ball and thereby puts a slice spin on the ball. This shot also can be played out of traps when a quick stop is necessary, only here the ball is played off the left foot so that a cushion of sand is taken before the ball is struck.

As I have said, I prefer always to take a putter out of a trap if there is no lip on the overhang or if the sand is not too soft.

However, there are times when you must play an explosion shot which will pop the ball up into the air.

Here the stance is slightly open, meaning that the left foot is withdrawn from the line of flight slightly, and the ball is played off the left heel with the face of the club opened. Under these conditions, you must be certain that your feet are firmly implanted in the sand.

A smooth, unhurried swing is the basis of the good trap shot. One of the most important factors is a full follow through.

Grounding your club in a trap before hitting the ball is against the rules and calls for a penalty. However, you can tell the texture of the sand as you walk into the trap and as you firmly plant your feet. In normal sand you will hit anywhere from one to two inches behind the ball but if the sand is exceptionally soft then you hit slightly closer to the ball. In the case where the sand is hard or wet then you must strike farther away from the ball, as much as three or four inches behind it, and drive the clubhead on through the sand in a full follow through.

PUTTING

Putting is a highly individualistic matter. Even on the professional golf tour there are countless ways in which the players putt.

Some use the interlocking grip, some the overlapping grip, others the reverse overlap, and still others even putt cross-handed.

On the whole they fall into two categories. One is the wrist and arm putter while the other contains the shoulder putters, who keep the hands and wrists immovable and merely swing the shoulders to make contact with the ball.

You will notice all types and sizes of putters, even on the pro tour, with some using the mallet, others the blade putter, and there even have been those who use the pendulum type of putter which is swung between the legs much like a croquet mallet.

How you stand, how you strike the ball, and what type of putter you use is strictly up to you.

Your putting, however, will be helped immeasurably if you learn to read the greens. The two major determining factors are the speed of the putt and the line over which it must travel.

The texture of the grass and the contour of the green are the two deciding factors.

Considering the grain of the grass, if the grass has been cut toward you this means that the blades of grass are leaning in your direction and the ball must be stroked more firmly than it would have to be struck if the grass was cut and leaning toward the hole.

One such condition, that in which the grass is bent away from you, can often be seen by the glossy sheen of the grass. On the other hand, if the grass has a darker appearance then, in all probability, it is bent toward you and the putt will have to be struck a bit more firmly.

Naturally, if your putt must follow a path which slopes to the left, you will have to putt up to the right to compensate for the downward pull of gravity. If the blades of grass are pointing up hill, however, even this slight resistance will prevent the ball from rolling off as much as if the blades of grass were pointing down hill. This means that the ball will break more slowly against the grain than it would with the grain.

Once having sized up the grain of the grass and the speed with which the putt must travel, you still must determine your line. This can be done much better by crouching down several feet behind your ball and inspecting the course over which it must travel to the hole.

Keep in mind, however, that there is one thing which most good putters all have in common. This is that they keep their head and body perfectly still while making their stroke.

But how you do it is completely up to you and you alone. First of all select a comfortable stance and grip and then it is a matter of practice. Because only through having confidence in both your stance and grip will you be able to pop it into the hole. And that, believe me, is the name of the game.

MY ALL-TIME TOP TEN

I presume that in ranking the ten best players of all time in order I probably shall create a storm of controversy and possibly, in the process, put quite a few indentations into many people's feelings. All I can say is that I mean no offense to anyone and yet, having seen all of these players over the years and having played with most of them, I consider myself fully qualified to make such an analysis.

It doesn't require much imagination to acknowledge that there will be irritated snorts and howls of indignation from various quarters and that "presumptuous" well may be the mildest word fired in my direction. How, it conceivably will be demanded, can anyone attempt to compare players who were champions with the hickory shafts of the past against the steel shaft breed of today? Doesn't this man realize that the early heroes had no sand iron or pitching wedge?

Naturally I realize the hazards at hand in attempting any such evaluation. Yet I honestly believe that a ranking such as this is fair and equitable when you take into consideration all the facets that make a champion and how he plays various types of shots. Sam Snead never carried a two wood, yet he can be rated on this club simply through the manner in which he played the driver on one side and the three wood on the other.

Laud the players of previous eras, if you will, for what they accomplished without a pitching wedge or a sand iron. Yet they can be assayed on these clubs if you observed, as I did, how they played these types of shots with the implements they had at hand.

Actually, there were compensations for each camp and I am not too certain but what the earlier players didn't have the best of it on an overall basis. Certainly the clubs are better today because they are matched as carefully as a jeweler grading a string of pearls.

Yet, let's consider two other angles. Those of previous eras played with a smaller, heavier ball. This was a distinct advantage because the ball they used gave them more distance and was much easier to putt. Take into consideration, too, that your earlier stars in a major event had only eight or ten rivals to beat because the field of top-flight competitors with a chance to win was so small in those times. Every tournament today is overloaded with talent and any one of fifty or more players can crash through to victory.

Which, considering the record and my own evalu-

Jack Nicklaus, Pebble Beach, California, 1961 (Wide World)

ation system, has to make Jack Nicklaus my careful choice as golf's greatest player of them all and only time will tell how far in front of the field he finally finishes.

I mentioned that I had figured out my own system of evaluation. To arrive at this you will note, in the accompanying chart, that I give ten points for perfection, or as close as we humans can come to perfection, with each of sixteen possible clubs. To this I have added fifteen points for concentration, fifteen points for aggressiveness, and ten points for positive thinking. These three qualities, I contend, round out the perfect golfer and provide a total point score of two hundred as the best anyone could possibly get.

No golfer is absolutely perfect, never has been, or ever will be.

But on my system, and on my personal observation, Nicklaus comes out as the best ever with a score of 193.

It is, to my reckoning, one single point ahead of the immortal Bobby Jones, whom I rank at 192 points. Ben Hogan is my third choice at 189; Arnold Palmer, fourth at 188 and still able to climb in the future; Walter Hagen and Byron Nelson are tied for fifth at 184; Sam Snead, the seventh greatest at 179; Gene Sarazen, eighth at 172; Tommy Armour, ninth at 171; and Gary Player, tenth with 170 points.

I have had to bypass a number of true golfing greats in formulating this all-time top ten and I feel that they deserve mention. This list certainly should include such as Cary Middlecoff, who won two U. S. Open Championships and was a runner-up in a third as well as winning the Masters; Ralph Guldahl, who captured two U. S. Opens back to back; Julius Boros, who won two U. S. Opens; Jimmy Demaret, a three-time Masters champion; Lawson Little, who won two United States and British Amateurs back to back as well as the U. S. Open Championship; Craig Wood, who won both the U. S. Open and the Masters; Jackie Burke, who captured both the P. G. A. and the Masters; Tony Lema, who in 1964 won the British Open and three other championships within a six-week period; Doug Ford, another Masters and P. G. A. champion; Chick Evans, who won two United States amateur titles as well as the United States Open; and Francis Ouimet, the first amateur to win the United States Open and who added two United States Amateur Championships to his list of titles.

There are a great number of other stars who, of course, would have to be considered in almost any list of great golfing competitors, but you have to draw the line somewhere.

There has been much aversion, both vocal and printed, in the last few years to the title "Big Three," meaning Nicklaus, Palmer, and Player. However, consider that they rank in my analyses as the only current younger stars in the all-time top ten. It would seem, definitely, to be a phrase very difficult to contradict.

Nicklaus' record is almost unbelievable to me con-

MY ALL-TIME TOP TEN

	JACK NICKLAUS	BOBBY JONES	BEN HOGAN	ARNOLD PALMER
DRIVER	10	10	10	8
TWO WOOD	10	10	8	8
THREE WOOD	10	10	10	8
FOUR WOOD	10	10	8	8
ONE IRON	10	10	8	10
TWO IRON	10	10	10	10
THREE IRON	10	10	10	10
FOUR IRON	10	10	10	10
FIVE IRON	10	9	10	10
SIX IRON	10	9	10	10
SEVEN IRON	10	8	10	10
EIGHT IRON	10	6	10	8
NINE IRON	8	10	8	8
PITCHING WEDGE	8	10	10	10
SAND IRON	7	10	9	10
PUTTER	10	10	8	10
CONCENTRATION	15	15	15	15
AGGRESSIVENESS	15	15	15	15
POSITIVE THINKING	10	10	10	10
TOTALS	193	192	189	188

(*Rated on 10 points as perfection with each of 16 possible club plus 15 points each for concentration and aggressive-*

WALTER HAGEN	BYRON NELSON	SAM SNEAD	GENE SARAZEN	TOMMY ARMOUR	GARY PLAYER
7	10	10	8	10	8
7	10	10	8	10	8
7	10	10	10	10	10
7	8	8	10	10	10
6	10	10	6	10	8
10	10	10	8	8	8
10	10	10	8	8	9
10	10	10	9	8	9
10	10	10	9	8	9
10	8	10	8	7	9
10	8	8	8	7	9
10	10	8	8	7	9
10	10	8	9	6	9
10	10	10	10	6	9
10	7	10	10	8	8
10	8	10	8	8	10
15	10	10	10	15	10
15	15	10	15	15	10
10	10	7	10	10	8
184	184	179	172	171	170

ness and 10 points for positive thinking. The perfect player would have a score of 200.)

sidering the tender age at which he was sky-rocketed to the top of the professional golfing heap. Jack did not turn pro until November 1961 and as this is written, while he is only twenty-five, his triumphs against fantastic fields include two United States Amateur Championships, the United States Open, the P. G. A. and two Masters Championships.

Jack took the United States Amateur in 1959 and again in 1961. In 1960, as an amateur, he finished second in the United States Open only two shots behind Arnold Palmer, quite a feat when you consider that no amateur has won the Open Championship since Johnny Goodman turned the trick way back in 1933.

During his first year as a professional, Nicklaus beat Palmer in a play-off for the 1962 United States Open Championship and on top of that won the Portland and Seattle Opens as well as the televised World Series of Golf. The next year, 1963, Jack took the Masters and the P. G. A. as well as the Tournament of Champions, Palm Springs, the Sahara Invitational, and the televised World Series of Golf for the second year in a row.

I go on reciting his triumphs because to me it is a great clinching point. So consider that in 1964 he won the Australian Open, the Phoenix Open, the Tournament of Champions again, the Whitemarsh Open, the Portland Open and was second in both the P. G. A. and the British Open.

Take into consideration too that he and Palmer represented Uncle Sam in the Canada Cup and International Trophy matches and while they teamed to win the Canada Cup for the United States on both occasions, playing head-to-head against Palmer for individual honors, Nicklaus won the International Trophy both times.

Then, starting in 1965, Nicklaus was little less than sensational in winning the Masters for the second time. Ben Hogan had toured the Augusta National course to win the Masters in 1953 with a record of 274. Everyone agreed that this was a mark which never could be erased.

All that Nicklaus did in April of 1965 was fire rounds of 67-71-64-69—271. It shattered Hogan's record by three shots and the closest man to Nicklaus when it all was over was nine shots behind him.

All of this, as I said, at the age of twenty-five.

If all goes well for him, I feel quite certain that before he is through Nicklaus will have completely rewritten the golfing history books.

I say this because in all my forty-five years of golf never have I seen anyone break into the game of golf in such a resounding manner as he did. His only weakness, if there is any at all, is in his short game with the nine iron and the wedges. If this young man learns how to handle those clubs as well as he does the rest of the tools in his bag I am quite certain that before he is through he will compile an absolutely untouchable record which will stand through the golfing ages.

I have never seen a player in my life who hits the

ball as long as Nicklaus does with such amazing accuracy. There have been a number of mileage hitters in the past such as Jimmy Thomson and George Bayer of more recent vintage but while they had the Nicklaus length they lacked his awesome control. There is a saying, "You drive for show but you putt for dough."

This is a flagrant fallacy. For the drive has tremendous influence on what you do from there on to the green. The 1965 Masters was an outstanding example.

I recall when Hogan won at Augusta, and broke the record with his 274 that everyone agreed, as I remarked, his record never possibly could be broken.

Nicklaus not only broke this record by three strokes but as I said actually ran away from the field to win by nine big strokes.

How great can you get?

Concerning the matter of long driving, the so-called 300-yard drive is strictly a matter of down hill with the wind behind you. On the dead flat, in a dead calm, nobody hits the ball 300 yards.

The U. S. Golf Association measured the drives of all competitors on two flat holes during the 1964 U. S. Open Championship at Congressional Country Club in Washington, D. C. The overall average for this all-star field was 252 yards. Nicklaus on these two holes was the longest hitter in the field and averaged 269 yards.

Bobby Jones is, of course, a golf legend who will live as long as the game is played.

His unmatched feat of 1930 in which he compiled

the fabled "Grand Slam" of winning both the United States and British Open and Amateur Championships never will be repeated.

I insist it never can be repeated because no amateur could hope to cope with the vast and talented professional fields of today enough to win both the United States and British Open Championships.

Jones retired at twenty-eight, immediately after the "Grand Slam," with four United States Opens, three British Opens, five United States Amateurs, and one British Amateur to his credit. Who can say what he might have gone on to accomplish? Yet, against today's field, I doubt that his record would have been quite so gaudy.

Undoubtedly Jones is regarded by many as the greatest of them all and I'll not quarrel with their feelings on the matter.

While he never used the pitching wedge and sand iron as we know them today, I give him top rating with these clubs because of his artistry around the greens. I always felt that his weakness, if I may call an infinitesimal fault, was with the shorter irons and here I am calling them as I saw them. I am not saying that Jones was not a magnificent player and in many ways the greatest of them all.

Yet I do feel that man to man and field to field, Nicklaus already has proved himself a shade the best.

In rating my top ten, I am not only concerned with the championships which these men won. This does not mean, in placing Ben Hogan in third place, that I am not cognizant of the fact that he won the United States Open four times, the P. G. A. twice, the Masters twice, and the British Open in his one effort.

Ben was undoubtedly the greatest of his era, and yet I felt there were certain flaws spotted throughout his game. This weakness developed because in his younger and hungrier days he had been a chronic hooker. As he progressed he played it only one way, left to right, guarding against that left side even when an aggressive attack demanded a hook.

When a man refuses the challenge, or is unable to meet it, the weaknesses must show up here and there down the line.

There will be many people who will feel that Palmer should stand higher than the fourth position in which I rate him on his records of being the only four-time winner of the Masters as well as having won the United States Amateur, the United States Open, and two British Opens.

Palmer certainly is one of the most exciting players I have ever seen in the game of golf and proof of this is his ever present, always vociferous gallery alluded to phonetically as "Arnie's Army."

Palmer has some of his best years ahead of him and has an enviable record, yet to me he possesses weaknesses which make me rate him as I do.

I do not consider Palmer a great driver or wood player, by any means. He hits it long but he is erratic.

Toney Penna, Bing Crosby and Frank Sinatra, Palm Springs, 1963 (Milt Jones)

It must be conceded that Palmer doesn't let it bother him as much as it would bother a majority of other players.

The reason is his aggressiveness and the magnetic manner in which he is always on the attack when playing a hole. Palmer to me is the Silky Sullivan of modern golf, although he doesn't fold in the big ones like the California wonder horse.

Still, he is guilty too often of spraying his shorter irons, demonstrating a definite lack of technique and "touch" with them. What saves him is that he is one of the greatest scramblers of all time and can play almost any type of shot around the greens with just about any club in the bag.

Merely ranking a man on the number of titles he has won, as I pointed out earlier, would be a travesty. Otherwise I should have to rank Walter Hagen higher than the fifth place which I give him on my all-time top ten due to the fact that he won five P. G. A. Championships, four British Opens, and two United States Opens.

Hagen rates with me as probably the slickest and soundest strategist ever to play golf. His mannerisms and his analyses of a shot were masterpieces.

"Sir Walter" won five P. G. A. Championships at match play and his swashbuckling performances had as much to do with eliminating his frustrated and outgeneraled opponents as did his shots. Still, analyzing a particular shot and getting the most out of it was one of his great assets. One of his weaknesses, of course, was the fact that he never devoted much time for practice and perfecting various shots but simply took them as they came and pulled them off with sheer talent. Hagen was one of the first men I ever saw use a putter out of a sand trap. His wood play left a great deal to be desired and yet his iron play was as fine as any I've ever been privileged to see, especially in the wind.

Byron Nelson, whom I rank as sixth, in the mid 1940s was the scourge of the fairways. He finished in the money in 113 tournaments, won eleven tournaments in a row at one stage, and captured two Masters, the United States Open, and two P. G. A. titles.

Nelson was to me the "Seabiscuit" of golf. That record of eleven straight tournament wins will, I believe, stand for a good long time, possibly forever with the ever larger fields which are more highly talented from year to year.

Nelson's long iron game was of unsurpassing brilliance. His most damning weakness was in sand play. His putting also left a great deal to be desired for, while he was great at times, he could be absolutely atrocious on the greens at other times. Byron's concentration on the golf course was a sometime thing, also, and was so upsetting to him that on some occasions if he started badly he would walk right off the golf course.

I can place Sam Snead no higher than seventh on my all-time top ten and it serves to point up my contention that you cannot rank a man simply on victories alone.

Otherwise, Sam might have to be ranked as the greatest of them all. For, how can you fault a man who has won at least 115 tournaments including the P. G. A. Championship three times, the Masters three times, the British Open and, after he passed the fifty-year-old mark, won two P. G. A. Senior titles in a row.

Sam is one of the very finest swingers and stylists of all time and when Snead timed his swing perfectly he was one of the longest drivers in the history of the game.

One deficit of major importance to those who count titles would be that Snead never was able to win the United States Open Championship.

I have played often with Sam and his short irons have never equaled the rest of his game. Yet I must hold that his greatest combined weaknesses were in his inability to concentrate, a lack of aggressiveness, and the shortage in his makeup to think positively. Sam was so uncertain of his own judgment that he pilloried his caddies if they could not tell him what type shot to play or what club to hit. When a top drawer professional has to ask his bag bearer to club him it is a tip-off on mental distress and uncertainty. If Snead hadn't been so fabulous in so many other departments, including sheer talent, you might almost wonder how he ever won one tournament, let alone 115.

Start judging players primarily on the championships they have won and certainly Gene Sarazen would have to rank much higher than the eighth place which I must award him.

Gary Player, San Francisco, 1962 (Wide World)

The chunky Sarazen at twenty became the youngest winner of the P. G. A. Championship, and captured it a total of three times as well as winning the Masters, the United States Open two times, and the British Open.

Sarazen started in a blaze of glory and later in his career suffered a terrific slump. At this point he displayed a bulldog courage as well as know-how to rebuild his entire game. During this period he came up with an instrument that still is in use today, an extraordinarily heavy training club. With this Gene changed his swing and also was one of the few players of that era who successfully made the transition to steel shafts and came back to capture major championships.

Even later on in years when he was past fifty he went on to win the P. G. A. Seniors Championship. You would undoubtedly have to consider him one of the very greatest, although no better than eighth according to my calculations. Being ultracritical in these ratings I fault Gene primarily off the tee and in his iron play and this being the way my figures come out, I'll just have to ride along with them.

Sarazen, it must be recorded, was one of the most aggressive players ever, a man who attacked a golf course with reckless abandon. Yet a part of his failing was a lack of patience to fight it out. If Sarazen went bad, he went bad. There was no happy medium with Gene: he was either a winner or a loser. Strangely enough, Gene's concentration was of the icy Hogan variety and yet when it came to positive thinking he wasn't quite up to standard.

There probably will be more stormy weather for Toney Penna for placing Tommy Armour no better than ninth on my list.

For I have played more golf with Armour than with anyone else I have ever known.

Tommy, who won the United States and British Opens as well as the P. G. A. Championship, was a solid technician and a peerless perfectionist. Tommy analyzed every shot rather slowly but when he made up his mind he was quite sure as to what the shot should look like and how it should come off.

Armour remains entrenched in my mind as one of the finest wood club players of all time. Never have I seen anyone who could manipulate a driver through the fairway as well as Tommy. In every phase of the woods, the driver, the brassie, the spoon or the four wood, he was unbeatable. His long irons were excellent too, but I would have to consider Armour a much better wood player than an iron player.

Surprisingly enough, he is remembered as "The Iron Master," a tag hung on him by sports writers, and yet I do not believe that his iron play ever could compete with his wood shots. It was the wood shots to the most advantageous places in the fairway which made his iron play to the green seem so deadly. This was simply because he had set himself up for the easiest approach shot possible.

Gary Player, who earns my tenth spot, is the only player besides Ben Hogan and Gene Sarazen to win all four of the major championships, the United States and British Open, the P. G. A. and the Masters.

These four championships today are considered by the professionals as the modern "Grand Slam" if accomplished in one year. Personally I doubt that anyone will ever make it.

Gary's main problem originally was his lack of distance against the bombers of today and nobody ever worked harder to get the maximum out of a minimum. He did calisthenics and worked with weights and has improved his swing and his entire game a great deal. I rate him highest with his fairway woods and his putter—the clubs which won the United States Open title for him in 1965.

It would be unkind to say that the little South African has been able to get the most out of the least. For, after all, it isn't too much of the "least" to rank tenth among all of the legendary figures who have attained greatness on the fairways of the world.

MIND YOUR MANNERS

Tournament golf has become a major industry, with various types of events following the sun all the way across the country and even into foreign lands on almost every weekend of the year.

It appears to be, on the surface, a very glamorous life. Certainly it is different and the professional players enjoy it or they would not do it.

Yet you must take into consideration that the professionals dash madly by car, plane, and train in a hectic and never-ending pursuit of the elusive dollar and it is a grim, wearing business in which the constant travel alone is enough to drive a man to distraction.

This is compounded by innumerable other nerve-racking problems. These range from lost baggage to car trouble to inability to obtain air reservations, errant laundry and cleaning, straying hotel reservations, frequent physical upsets from ever-changing food and water, and, during those infrequent periods when they are fortunate enough to take along the family, the added problems posed as any traveler knows of caring for a wife and children when away from the regular routine of home life. While the younger bachelors of the brassie do not have this added chore, this vagabond existence still is no picnic when you consider all the frustrating facets with which they are involved.

What I am building up to is that I believe it is about time that something was said to hammer these points home to the public in the hope that the galleries, as welcome as they are, will refrain from stomping on the players' nerve ends.

I'm referring to gallery etiquette.

Tournament golf is packed to the brim with unbelievable tension. The competitors played for roughly $2,500,000 in 1965. That sounds like and it is a tremendous amount of money. Yet you must take into consideration that it costs roughly about $8,000 a year for a player to meet his expenses on tour, and that's figuring it close to his vest. This includes meals, lodging, transportation, caddies' fees, clothing and its care, and a thousand and one other expenditures.

Some players are sponsored on the tour, meaning that a group of friends pay them so much money per week to cover their expenses. For this they return to their backers a certain specified percentage of their winnings. But the majority go it alone and when each shot is translated into hundreds of dollars, or even thousands of dollars, the strain becomes almost unimaginable. This is true even in the case of the "Haves" as well as in the cases of the "Have Nots."

The name stars of course are battling to stay on top because additional victories mean that they will remain in continued demand for endorsements, exhibitions and such, all of which add up to increased income. The younger players are fighting desperately to advance from the "Have Not" class to a place at or near the top of the money-winning bracket.

Thus even the most successful tournament stars are always conscious of the pack breathing hot on their heels and their task is complicated by the fact that they draw the largest, jostling, ever-shifting, running, cheering galleries as a constant panoramic background. Too often these masses of spectators following the stars also have an upsetting effect on the unknown players fighting old man par in their pursuit of fame and fortune.

Because five thousand fans walking along with an Arnold Palmer or a Jack Nicklaus can completely ignore the fact that on an adjoining fairway young Mr. Unknown is trying lonesomely to play a shot which he hopes will get him onto the money list and earn him a check he needs so desperately. Often, at this crucial moment, the thundering herd will swarm down past him, around him, or over him in its hypnotized march in the wake of the stars.

It is a tough way of life in a glass pressure cooker and from top to bottom they all fight this nerve-shattering tension.

All of them feel it and I can give you a few classic examples.

First let us consider, for instance, the case of Byron Nelson. He was one of the game's most consistent winners, a tall, seemingly aloof man who always appeared as if he would be completely unconcerned and undismayed if, while playing a course in Iowa, a herd of elephants ambled out of an adjacent cornfield. Yet Byron often was physically ill before he teed off in a major tournament. Outwardly he would seem to be completely at ease. Inwardly he bubbled like a pot of stew boiling on the front burner.

Billy Casper teeing off on the final hole of the United States Open Championship with the prize within his grasp appeared on the surface to be the most placid man in the whole wide world. Inwardly, he has admitted, the crowds bothered him tremendously and often he was so tense the night before a tournament that he could not sleep a wink.

You would think that burly Mike Souchak, a former football star at Duke University, long since had become accustomed to the shifting kaleidoscope of a watching mass of humanity. But even big Mike knew the jitters which come from the almost intolerable pressure of being a miser with your strokes.

One of the prime gallery victims of all time has been

Tommy Bolt. He has for a long time had the reputation of possessing a highly explosive temper and of being a man who would throw a club at the drop of a double bogey. There were those who followed him around not only waiting for him to blow his top but hoping he would. Then, when the moment of unquenchable frustration came, as it does for every player at some time or other, they would yell: "Throw it, Tommy."

"I wish they would realize," he once said, "that they are taking the bread right out of my mouth."

Playing golf for a living can become a man's private torture chamber. There is no more significant analysis than that once made by Bobby Jones, and adding even greater import to his words is the fact that he was an amateur concerned only with honors and not with the added necessity of needing to win to pay his bills.

Jones made the differentiation that there are two kinds of golf: every-day golf and tournament golf.

The "Emperor" said that it was rare for him to eat even a restricted breakfast on the mornings in which he was to play a tournament round. And even on those occasions when he could eat, he did well to finish a strip of bacon and a cup of black coffee.

Jones described it as "subjective nerve-tension" and, pointing up the added wear and tear of physical as well as nervous tension—which undoubtedly go hand in hand—came to the point eventually where he never practiced at all the day before a tournament but rested and spent the entire day reading in bed if he could.

It must be obvious to all that the professionals who labor under these kinds of pressure, and tournament golf is grinding, grueling work, should be given every possible consideration by those in the gallery.

For these reasons, I would like to make the following suggestions for comportment while attending a tournament:

1. Do not be guilty of loud conversation or laughter even though you are outside the deep ring of spectators around a green because sounds carry unusually far on a golf course and one voice can be more upsetting to a player and to his concentration than a loud concentrated roar from a nearby green.

2. Be silent and motionless when a player is taking his stance and throughout his stroke.

3. Give the players plenty of room. Do not expect a man to shoot down a narrow lane of goggle-eyed faces. You are not only disturbing him but you also are courting injury, because nobody is infallible with a golf club.

4. Do not shout "Down in front!"

5. If the gallery is large, kneel if you are in the front row as a courtesy to those standing behind you.

6. Avoid applauding until it is merited and do not make it obvious if you favor one player over another. This is exceedingly unsportsmanlike.

7. Walk, do not run, or you may start a stampede in which somebody could be hurt.

8. Be fair to players who do not have galleries and respect the fact that they too are trying to win.

9. Stay behind the ropes and the white lines. They are put there for a purpose.

10. Walk around traps and bunkers, never through them.

11. Walk around greens, never across them.

12. Do not start charging to the next tee for a vantage spot just because your particular favorite has putted out. Give the other players with him a sporting chance.

Going even further in this matter of sportsmanship, it concerns me greatly that even in casual play I have noticed in too many quarters a general breakdown of golfing etiquette, by which I mean an increasing lack of consideration for others.

Now I do not say that you shouldn't enjoy yourself, for this is a fun game. Still, a golf course is not the place where the eardrum should be battered like feeding time at the zoo.

I can see no reason for shouting from one side of the fairway to the other or for emitting a blood-curdling whoop when you happen to hit a good shot or manage to hole a long putt. The reasoning should be obvious. The chances are that you will be disturbing another player on an adjoining hole just as he is making his shot.

In this day and age of extremely crowded courses, it is a sign of good manners to delay teeing off until those ahead of you are well out of range. All it requires is that you wait a few moments longer and thereby eliminate the possibility of hurting someone. A golf ball can cause a thumping lump on a person's head, or do even more damage. It happens, unfortunately, almost every day.

Crowded courses also make it mandatory, if you happen to be a slow player and find that those immediately behind you constantly are standing around waiting, to wave faster players on through. The few moments that they will require to play through certainly are inconsequential and the smiling thanks you receive will be payment in full as you realize that you have helped make someone else's day more enjoyable.

Concerning this too general dismissal of the fact that other players are being held up, play is speeded all around if on a short hole where others may be waiting behind you, upon reaching the green you will stand back and wave for them to hit their tee shots. In this manner you can putt out while they are moving toward the green and you will be following your next tee shot down the fairway before they are off of the green you have just abandoned.

Another inconsiderate practice I have observed is the too general habit of taking a few practice putts after one holes out while those behind are kept waiting.

What some people refer to as "Gamesmanship" but really is an unsporting attempt to upset on opponent, is unfortunately practiced on a rather wide scale. Your own companions will vastly appreciate your thoughtfulness if you do not stand too close, and restrain yourself from taking practice swings, or talking and moving about while they are hitting. This is a gentleman's game and a gentleman remains silently and motionlessly off to the side, preferably facing the hitter, if possible. If you are behind the man playing his shot, it can create in him the feeling that you might be too close and in the process upset his concentration. By your example you will be instilling in others this same thoughtfulness for you when you are hitting your shot.

No one has to be told that in golf it is the rule that the man who is the farthest away from the hole shoots first. Yet I frequently have observed those who happen to be playing with a slower or less able person demonstrate extreme ill manners by walking impatiently ahead to their ball, hit their shot, and then gallop on toward the green while their companion was left far in their wake. They have failed to take into consideration that they could be ruining the other man's day by instilling in him a feeling that they were scornful of his inability.

One of the most annoying denizens of the fairway is the fellow who incessantly tells raucous jokes. This type chatters on and on with his story even while you are addressing your ball, feeling possibly, if you want to give him the benefit of the doubt, that he is far enough away so that his voice will not bother you. But the odds are a dozen to one that he'll reach his punch line just as you are at the top of your backswing. This creature naturally laughs the loudest at his own jokes and the resulting cackle as you start your downswing can be completely devastating to your shot.

The time for jokes is when you're walking from the

green to the next tee or when you reach the locker room. It is well to remember that loud laughter carries a long way across the open spaces of a golf course and, I'll say it again, you could be disturbing other players on adjoining holes.

Those of us who regularly compete in tournaments have had to attempt to condition ourselves to sudden noises and diverting movement in the gallery and yet no one ever manages to become completely shockproof.

A case in point was that of Mike Souchak in the 1960 United States Open Championship at Cherry Hills in Denver. Mike was leading the tournament as he came to the eighteenth hole in the third round with another round facing him after lunch. Mike was playing well and there was no reason to think that he might not go on to win the championship.

But as he teed off on the eighteenth hole, right at the top of his backswing a spectator snapped his picture. It threw Souchak's whole swing out of gear and he walloped the ball out of bounds. The resulting penalty shortened his lead but, worse than that, Mike was so upset that he was unable to recover his composure. Mike's game fell apart and he lost one of golf's most coveted championships, I am convinced, because of that lone spectator's action.

All of this was due, as I am attempting.to show you, because of a thoughtless act.

As another example there is the unknown player who

Toney Penna, Plum Hollow, Detroit, Michigan, June 20, 1947
(Wide World)

happens to be paired with a Jack Nicklaus or an Arnold Palmer. Both of these great players always have a large gallery intent on watching them.

You can pity the poor fellow playing with them if, for example, Palmer putts out first and the unknown still has his putt to make. A good portion of the gallery immediately starts a stampede to get a position at the next tee. The fellow playing with him has to be distracted tremendously by this mass movement and crescendo of noise.

In this connection I must pay tribute to Tommy Bolt for his thoughtfulness in such an instance during the 1958 United States Open Golf Championship at Tulsa. Tommy was playing with a much lesser known player in the final round and coming to the seventy-first and semifinal green he had the tournament all locked up. Naturally he had the day's greatest gallery with him.

Tommy putted out and the other player still had his putt to make. Regardless of the situation, the gallery immediately began to stampede toward the next tee for vantage spots on Tommy's final drive.

Bolt stood in the center of the green, raised his arms, and shouted: "Fore, please stand and give this man a chance to putt out."

It is to the credit of that gallery that it immediately realized its thoughtlessness and stood in stony and motionless silence while the other man putted out.

It is, if I may repeat, simply sheer thoughtlessness on the part of the spectators. Still, it can be translated into your own game if you heedlessly start walking off the green after you have holed out despite the fact that your playing partners still have to putt.

In this same department, I might add, always take extreme care when lining up your putt or in putting that you do not stand in someone else's line, meaning the path over which their putt must travel after you have putted. You would be surprised how many players neglect this little nicety in which, through your thoughtfulness, you are able to avoid setting up an invisible footprint which well could throw another person's putt off line.

Another "don't" in becoming a gentlemanly player certain to be highly regarded is not to hit your approach shot until those in front of you have completely left the green. As I said, another few seconds may prevent unnecessary injury. The delay is negligible and, to your own advantage, you will find that you are not hurrying your shot and, in all probability, spoiling it in the process.

Still another character who is vastly unappreciated on the golf course is the fellow with the long, sharp "needle" who uses what passes for wit in an attempt to upset you and cause you to dub your shots. This is, of course, another unnecessary type of "gamesmanship" practiced in reality by a poor sportsman who quickly winds up on the unwanted list. Compliment even your rival on a fine shot and you will be the recipient of warm, genuine camaraderie.

Climbing down off the lecturer's dais, I would like to make a few suggestions aimed at the spectator's comfort as well as to enhance his own enjoyment while watching a tournament.

You will find that you will enjoy the whole panorama of a golf tournament a great deal more if you will carry a pair of binoculars as well as a folding canvas stool or a shooting stick. With the binoculars, from an advantageous hill you may be able to take in three or four or even more holes and the stool will permit you to sit close along the ropes so that others behind you will have a better view of what is going on.

Another tip I would like to give the spectator is to wear a light cap or summer straw hat if you have been unexposed to very much sunshine. I have seen tournaments where, because of the blazing sun, the spectators have dropped like flies and have been carted off to the Red Cross tent to recover, in the process ruining their whole day.

Also you should wear comfortable footwear, and you will find rubber-soled shoes are much more convenient than spikes because you will not have to remove your shoes when you enter the clubhouse dining room.

If you are in one of those tremendously large galleries which crop up at major championships, and which seem to get larger almost by the month, you will find it helpful to leapfrog the holes for better viewing, jumping from—for an example—the third hole to the fifth hole and then to the seventh hole to beat the rush. It is better to see one half of the match comfortably instead of being trampled while seeing little or nothing.

But, in summing up, on the golf course as at home there is no substitute for good manners.

What I have attempted to convey here was summed up completely by John Henry Cardinal Newman in one sentence:

"It is almost a definition of a gentleman to say he is one who never inflicts pain."

All I can add to that is that pain comes in many forms on the golf course and that golf is a gentleman's game.

THE AUTHORS AND THEIR BOOK

TONEY PENNA, *born in Naples, Italy, January 15, 1908, immigrated to the United States when he was five years old. Since the late 1920s he has been involved in one phase or another of golf, from caddy to professional tournament champion to club designer, salesman and vice-president for the MacGregor Company, well-known makers of golf equipment. During his active tournament career he won the North-South Open, the Kansas City Open, the Richmond Open, the Atlanta Open and the Southeastern P.G.A. Championship. He finished third in the 1938 U.S. Open.*

OSCAR FRALEY, *national sports columnist, is author of the* Bill Stern story, A Taste of Ashes *(Holt, 1959) and the* Judge Crater story, The Empty Robe *(Doubleday, 1961). He is co-author of books on many subjects from cooking to the F.B.I. One of these latter books,* The Untouchables *(Messner, 1957), written with Eliot Ness, became a popular television series. The adventures of Eliot Ness were continued in* Four Against the Mob *(Popular Library, 1961), and later in* The Last of the Untouchables *(Popular Library, 1962), written with Paul Robsky. His two most recent collaborations are* Golf Pro for God *with Johnny Spence (Centaur House, 1965) and* The All Star Athletes Cook Book *(Centaur House, 1965).*

A CENTAUR HOUSE BOOK